# HOLLYWOOD
# POOLSIDE

NORMA SHEARER

# HOLLYWOOD

# POOLSIDE

## CLASSIC IMAGES OF LEGENDARY STARS

*frans evenhuis ≈ robert landau*

ANGEL CITY PRESS

**BONITA GRANVILLE AND JACKIE COOPER**

ANGEL CITY PRESS, INC.
2118 Wilshire Boulevard, Suite 880
Santa Monica, California 90403
(310) 395-9982
www.angelcitypress.com

HOLLYWOOD POOLSIDE
Copyright © 1997 by Frans Evenhuis and Robert Landau
Designed by Frans Evenhuis

First published in 1997 by Angel City Press
1 2 3 4 5 6 7 8 9 10
FIRST EDITION
ISBN 1-883318-02-5

Library of Congress Cataloging-in-Publication Data

Evenhuis, Frans 1946- and Robert Landau
    Hollywood poolside : classic images of legendary stars / by Frans
Evenhuis and Robert Landau. – 1st ed.
        p.   cm.
    Includes bibliographical references and index.
    ISBN 1–883318–02–5 (cloth)
    1. Motion picture actors and actresses—Portraits. 2. Swimming
pools.  I. Landau, Robert, 1953–   .  II. Title.
PN1998.2.E98  1997
791.43'028'0922—dc21                               97–4574
                                                                    CIP

For Cherié Evenhuis

 and Hulya Karadeniz

IDA LUPINO

*h o l l y w o o d   p o o l s i d e*

# CONTENTS

CLARA BOW

CONSTANCE BENNETT

GENE TIERNEY

RONALD REAGAN

13

GINGER ROGERS

14

TYRONE POWER

15

BETTE DAVIS

ALEXIS SMITH

BETTY GRABLE

JAYNE MANSFIELD

COVER: For **HUMPHREY BOGART** the model of his fifty-five-foot sailing ship *Santana* probably represents his greatest love after wife **LAUREN BACALL**. The yacht was purchased around the time Bogart was making *Key Largo* (1948) and was named after the boat in the movie. This homebody image of Bogey in his backyard pool stands in stark contrast to the tough guys he played on screen. After Bogart's long struggle playing villains and toughs, Warner Bros. took a chance casting him as a romantic lead in a routine production called *Casablanca* (1942). Sparks flew on and off the set when he met Bacall, a model-turned-actress making her debut opposite him in *To Have and Have Not* (1945). Bogart divorced his wife and made Bacall his fourth actress-wife. The pair starred in three more movies together and remained happily married until Bogart's death in 1957. Bacall has continued to work in films and on Broadway.

DUST JACKET FLAP: **CLAUDETTE COLBERT** takes in the view of the Hollywood landscape from the deck of her hillside pool. Colbert established herself as a star playing Nero's wife in Cecil B. DeMille epic *The Sign of the Cross* (1932). In a famous scene from that film, she bathes in a milk-filled pool. But she is best remembered for her portrayal of an heiress traveling incognito with a reporter, played by Clark Gable, in the Frank Capra classic *It Happened One Night* (1934). Colbert and Gable both won Oscars for their roles. Colbert enjoyed further success both on stage and on the screen through the mid-fifties, then retired to Barbados, where she died in 1996.

TITLE PAGE: **NORMA SHEARER**, see caption, page 94.

PAGE 6: **IDA LUPINO** poses at her Hollywood Hills home beside her new swimming pool. Lupino had accompanied her mother, British actress Connie Emerald, on a trip to London in 1933 where Connie was to audition for the lead in the film *The First Affaire* (1933). However, the film's director Allan Dwan found her a bit old and offered the part to her daughter instead. Lupino made five more movies that year in England, then signed a contract with Paramount, and her Hollywood career was off and running. Considered at first to be an "English Harlow," it wasn't until a few years later when she changed her hair from blond to its natural dark brown that her acting talents were taken seriously. Lupino had a long career, eventually expanding into screen writing and even trailblazing as one of the few female directors working in Hollywood in the fifties.

PAGES 8-9: **CLARA BOW**, see caption, page 59.

PAGES 10-11: With a hair stylist no doubt within arm's length, **CONSTANCE BENNETT** makes a splash in this fetching publicity shot. Having started a career at seventeen that was quickly gaining popularity, Bennett surprised Hollywood when she just as quickly gave it all up in 1925 to marry a wealthy steamship heir. She enjoyed a brief fling with the international society set, but when the marriage ended four years later, she returned to the screen. Her deep voice and comedic delivery helped establish her as a star. She appeared in films in the forties, and continued to perform on stage in the fifties. Bennett was also married to Gilbert Roland.

PAGE 12: **GENE TIERNEY** was still a teenager when she told her wealthy stockbroker father that she wanted to be an actress. He immediately formed a corporation devoted to developing and promoting his daughter's career. His efforts paid off when Darryl F. Zanuck spotted the exotic beauty in a Broadway production. Her film career at Fox began with routine roles but she soon became a hot property and was often cast opposite Fox's popular star Tyrone Power. Tierney left some extremely powerful film impressions in the murder mystery *Laura* (1944) directed by Otto Preminger, and in *Leave Her To Heaven* (1945), where her performance as a murderous seductress earned an Academy Award nomination. A perfect mannequin for a clothing designer, Tierney was married to Oleg Cassini from 1941 to 1952. She was later engaged to Rita Hayworth's ex, Aly Khan. When Khan's father nixed the wedding plans, she suffered a nervous breakdown and took several years to recover.

PAGES 13: **RONALD REAGAN**, see caption, page 100.

PAGES 14: Best known as Fred Astaire's dance partner, **GINGER ROGERS** was groomed for stardom at an early age. Encouraged by her mother, Rogers began singing and dancing lessons at age five, debuted professionally in vaudeville at fourteen, and appeared in Broadway musicals such as George Gershwin's *Girl Crazy*, before moving on to Hollywood. At RKO her association with Astaire began, leading to ten classic musicals. When the partnership ended, Rogers expanded her film career with both dramatic and comic roles, and was linked romantically with many Hollywood heavyweights including Rudy Vallee, Jimmy Stewart and Howard Hughes.

PAGE 15: **TYRONE POWER**, see caption, page 102.

PAGES 16-17: **BETTE DAVIS**, see caption, page 105.

PAGE 18: A Warner Bros. talent scout discovered **ALEXIS SMITH** at a college stage production. After signing with the studio, she appeared in a variety of leading lady roles throughout the forties and fifties, usually playing self-sufficient characters. Smith retired from movies at the end of the fifties but returned to the stage in the seventies as the star of the Broadway musical *Follies*. Based on her renewed success, she resumed her movie career, with *Jacqueline Susann's Once is Not Enough* in 1975, fifteen years after first retiring. Smith's marriage to Craig Stevens (known to TV audiences as "Peter Gunn") lasted for forty-nine years, until her death in 1993.

PAGE 19: **BETTY GRABLE**, see caption, page 97.

PAGE 20-21: **JAYNE MANSFIELD**, see captions, pages 106 and 112.

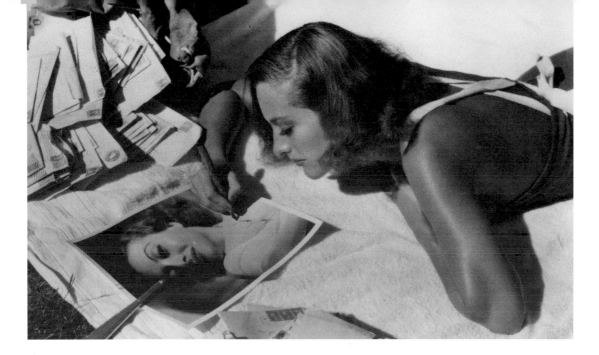

Pictured at poolside in 1933 serenely answering her fan mail, **JOAN CRAWFORD** was in reality going through a very complicated year. Although she had become a major star rivaling the popularity of Greta Garbo and Norma Shearer, her private life was in turmoil. Having suffered yet another miscarriage, her marriage to Douglas Fairbanks, Jr., was collapsing when she fell in love with her *Dancing Lady* (1933) co-star Clark Gable. The two had a fling, but Gable was already married and, according to Crawford, only interested in women who were "not too available."

# THANKS

Compiling material for *Hollywood Poolside* required a great deal of help from many sources. In our quest to locate pictures, we enlisted the help of several agencies and collections and we are most appreciative. We'd like to acknowledge the specific contributions and patience of Ron Harvey of the Everett Collection, Howard Mandelbaum of Photofest, Alan Reuben of Culver Pictures, Dick DeNeut of Globe Photos, Marc Wanamaker of Bison Archives, the staff and collection of the Academy of Motion Picture Arts & Sciences' Center for Motion Picture Study Margaret Herrick Library, and Sally Hall McManus of the Palm Springs Historical Society.

Alan and Sharon Waldman made invaluable contributions to the text and research, and important facts were supplied by Jeff Hyland, Marty Geimer and the staff of Hearst San Simeon State Historic Monument. We also want to thank Gary Gershaw and Sheri Mobley of Mobley Marketing Communications, Ann Flower of Warren Cowan and Associates, Jeff Wack and Nathan Wong for their Adobe Photoshop work, Gretchen and Graham Lewis for generously allowing use of their computers and pool, as well as the following indivituals: Dick Wells, Gene Trindl, Jeff Silverman, Jerry Lazar and Beth Vesel.

A very special thanks to our editors Paddy Calistro and Jean Penn for their enthusiasm, patience and prodding. And, finally, a nod of gratitude to the studios that produced the movies and employed the many anonymous photographers whose work preserved the history documented in this book.

While making the Preston Sturges film *Sullivan's Travels* in 1941, **VERONICA LAKE** and **JOEL McCREA** enjoyed a taste of the privileged life on the Janss family estate, where this scene was shot. If it hadn't been for her hairstyle, Lake might not have been quite as legendary. But that "peek-a-boo" do that almost obscured one eye became such a trend that she was one of the hottest stars of the early forties. At one point the War Department had to step in and ask her to change her style, since so many Rosie-the-Riveter types were adopting the look – semi-blinded by their tresses, workers' long hair easily got caught in machinery. Lake enjoyed some hits in which she was teamed with Alan Ladd, starting with *This Gun For Hire* (1942). Her love life was in the news when she dated Greek millionaire Aristotle Onassis and Hollywood tycoon Howard Hughes. By the end of the forties, however, her popularity declined and her career went awry. She filed for bankruptcy, dropped out and disappeared. In the sixties a journalist tracked her down in the bar of a New York hotel where she was serving drinks. By 1973, after a final failed attempt to jump-start her career, she died from hepatitis. McCrea's career was as hot as Lake's in the forties, when he had the lead in Alfred Hitchcock's *Foreign Correspondent* (1940) and Sturges' *The Palm Beach Story* (1942). After 1946 he appeared mostly in westerns. For McCrea, who had grown up in Hollywood helping early cowboy stars Tom Mix and William S. Hart with their horses, this represented the completion of a career circle.

# INTRODUCTION

Marilyn Monroe poses on the diving board of a Hollywood pool.
A young Ronald Reagan at his bare-chested, beefcake best mugs for
the camera just before taking a dip. Bogart and Bacall allow fans a
glimpse of their backyard poolside manner. A young Clint Eastwood,
in his pre-spaghetti western days, shows the world that he's just a
regular guy by cleaning his own pool.

*Hollywood Poolside* is a collection of rare photographs taken
between 1915 and 1965, from Hollywood's earliest days through
its Golden Age. Originally intended for the pages of America's
movie magazines and the international press, only some of
the photos made it into the slick journals. Nevertheless,
half a century or more after these celebrity shots came
out of the camera, these pictures collectively
comprise a chronicle of a world that looked every
bit as glamorous as it was.

Together, the new wealth generated by
the movies, the sunny climate and open
spaces of southern California created
a lifestyle that fascinated
the world.

**JEAN HARLOW** strikes
a pose in her BVD swimsuit,
which featured a rather
innocent round neckline
in front, a daring
extremely low-cut back.
It was the perfect design to
reflect her sex-kitten
image. Harlow got her break
as the heroine in Howard Hughes'
World War I epic *Hell's Angels*
(1930). Under contract to Hughes,
the platinum blonde developed a
reputation for playing coarse,
wise-cracking characters with a
vulnerable side, which also
paralleled her off-screen personality.
When Harlow moved to MGM in
1932, she became more refined,
developing into a sexy, sultry
comedienne. Nicknamed "Baby,"
she died suddenly of a cerebral
edema at age twenty-six.

Although it is located some two hundred forty miles north of Hollywood, the Neptune Pool at **HEARST CASTLE** is nonetheless one of the most famous and opulent pools in Hollywood lore. William Randolph Hearst first connected with the world of Hollywood in 1917 when he met and fell in love with a young starlet named Marion Davies. Not especially fond of the castle, Davies preferred to stay at the hundred-ten-room Santa Monica beach house that Hearst maintained for her. While guests at the castle included such dignitaries as Sir Winston Churchill, George Bernard Shaw and Calvin Coolidge, Davies was happiest when her Hollywood friends such as Charlie Chaplin, Mary Pickford, Gloria Swanson, Errol Flynn, Carole Lombard and young Jimmy Stewart came to visit. Fortunately, Hearst loved to be around the youthful movie crowd. He hired some of the stars to appear in Davies' movies, and he was known to hide new contracts under their plates at the dinner table. Guests had their choice of swimming in an indoor pool, or in the Greco-Roman style Neptune pool, which holds 345,000 gallons of water, and is filled (even today) with mountain spring water. The pool area has seventeen dressing rooms that could accommodate the forty to fifty guests Hearst usually entertained on weekends. Hearst himself was an accomplished swimmer and often went into the pool with one of his many pet dachshunds.

Rambling estates with swimming pools and tennis courts were as much a part of the Hollywood image as were fancy cars and flashy clothes. Initially only the movie moguls had all the trappings, but the kingpins of film quickly taught their studios that promoting their stars and the myth of Hollywood would generate more money. That entailed trumpeting glamorous lives spent in glamorous pursuits. Lounging at poolside was foremost among them.

Completed in 1912, the Spanish-style **BEVERLY HILLS HOTEL** looked liked an oasis in the bare, dusty terrain of its surroundings. The hotel, a huge success almost from the beginning, was packed with guests from the icy midwestern and eastern states. Many who came decided to stay and establish homes and businesses nearby. Soon the hotel sat in the middle of America's wealthiest neighborhood. The hotel's now legendary Polo Lounge opened in the thirties. Since swimming became Hollywood's favorite pastime, a huge swimming pool was added in 1935. By the forties, when this picture was taken, the "Pink Palace," as it was called, had become the ultimate playground of the rich and famous: the Astors, Vanderbilts, Fords, Rockefellers and Kennedys joined the likes of the Duke and Duchess of Windsor, the Prince and Princess of Monaco and the Queen of Holland. They all stayed at the hotel, mixing with Polo Lounge regulars such as John Barrymore, Marlene Dietrich, W.C. Fields, Marilyn Monroe, Orson Welles and Frank Sinatra, creating the movie-star appeal that gave the hotel its cachet.

Hollywood, whose business was to create and sell fantasies through motion pictures, quickly began its self-promotion work, and seized the swimming pool as an icon. What really set pools apart from the other trappings of extreme wealth – expensive cars, fine clothes, diamonds and pearls, exotic travel – was the unique opportunity a pool provided for flaunting the stars' wealth and sex appeal in a single photograph. Stars could be photographed around their pools clad in sexy, body-baring swimwear while still maintaining the veneer of respectability that comes from socially acceptable behavior, such as the pursuit of physical fitness or good clean family fun.

BELOW: The pool at the Beverly Hills Hotel, the site of many Hollywood happenings, appears in a scene from *Designing Women* (1957) with **LAUREN BACALL** and **GREGORY PECK** at poolside.

When Prince Aly Khan, the royal playboy, divorced **RITA HAYWORTH**, UPPER RIGHT, he was hoping to marry **GENE TIERNEY**, UPPER LEFT. Khan's father disapproved of the relationship and the break-up caused Tierney to have a nervous breakdown, leaving her despondent for years.

LOWER LEFT: On location in Kenya to film *Safari* (1956), **VICTOR MATURE** and **JANET LEIGH** kept cool with a playful plunge in the pool. But naturally, all wasn't as upbeat as this publicity shot might suggest. Aside from the intense heat, the cast and crew had to endure wild animals, windstorms, near disasters on stunt action scenes, stomach troubles and sleep interrupted by intruders. Hunters were eventually hired to guard the troupe at night, but on the trip Leigh picked up a tropical ailment that remained a nuisance for years.

LOWER RIGHT: Although she appeared in over seventy movies, major stardom eluded **ANITA LOUISE**. She began acting as a child on the stage, and concluded her career on television where she starred in *My Friend Flicka* (1956-57). Louise was married to Buddy Adler, who became head of Twentieth Century-Fox.

28

The pool actually assumed the status of an additional room of the house and became a focal point not only for exercise, but for gatherings both formal and familial, a spot for socializing, exercising, playing, tanning and even occasionally for quiet contemplation. The stars – along with friends, family, other stars, or sometimes even all alone – swam laps, made swan dives, held parties, lounged, read scripts or just horsed around.

These poolside events were dutifully recorded by the press, especially since they provided an excellent opportunity to photograph stars in skimpy bathing costumes and show off their bodies and perfect tans. Often the photographer would set up some goofy, semi-spontaneous situation or pose a starlet in a corny stance. Still, in contrast to today's over-styled and pretentious magazine layouts, even the most contrived photographs from this period have an air of guileless innocence and downright playfulness. These images of the glamorous "real life" adventures of movies stars "at home and play" emanated from the public relations machinery at the studios – a slew of press agents were busy creating another form of mythology from a mythic land called Hollywood.

**JACKIE COOPER**, a child star of the thirties, appeared in many "Our Gang" episodes and starred in hit films such as *Skippy* (1931), *The Champ* (1931) and *Treasure Island* (1934). By the forties, when this photograph was taken of him clowning around in the pool with another child star of the thirties, **BONITA GRANVILLE**, Cooper was no longer in demand for films. Moving into television, he worked successfully as an actor, director and producer. Cooper resumed his movie career in the seventies and eighties with a recurring role in all four *Superman* movies. Granville, who received an Oscar nomination for the film *These Three* (1936), retired from acting in 1947, married a wealthy businessman and became producer of the endearing *Lassie* television series.

The pools at Hollywood hotels were more than just places to swim and relax. They became focal points for social gatherings and casual business meetings, places to see and to be seen. Visiting dignitaries and actors who did not make their homes in Hollywood often rented hotel bungalows for extended stays. The "swimming plunge" at the Ambassador Hotel, BELOW, was considered the most beautiful pool in the West in its day. That's **MARY PICKFORD** standing on the right, behind a row of bathing beauties. The Ambassador also housed the famous Coconut Grove nightclub and was near many swank restaurants and night spots.

Not only did the stars cooperate, they seemed to enjoy their roles in defining the good life. At the beginning of the twentieth century, when "stars at home" photos first began circulating in the world press, they cast an almost mythological spell on a generation of people who lived in cold, difficult environments and were struggling to make ends meet with tedious jobs and simple lives. The pictures of semi-naked idols leisurely drinking in the sun symbolized the ultimate expression of the impossible dream.

Hollywood, the actual locale, and Hollywood, the movie Mecca, grew up together, feeding off one another as both gained status. Real-estate developers, determined to lure easterners to southern California, did their best to promote Los Angeles and its environs as the "new Eden." Who could resist an oasis of swaying palm trees and gentle ocean breezes, year-round sunshine and fertile valleys of orange groves all nestled within view of snow-capped mountain ranges?

ABOVE: In the heyday of Hollywood, it was common for studios to sign up hundreds of attractive girls to long-term, low-paying contracts. Promoted as future stars, these so-called "starlets," like the Columbia beauties pictured here, rarely made it to the top. OPPOSITE: Bathing beauties, like these girls at the La Jolla Swim & Tennis Club, were also hopeful that they might be discovered by the studios' roving talent scouts.

The adventurers who composed the blossoming movie-making industry liked the idea of a place where a man with a little gumption could escape the oppression of harsh winters and restrictive lifestyles, reinvent himself in any way he saw fit and maybe even strike it rich. Then clustered around New York, movie makers were sometimes squeezed by the powerful Motion Picture Patents Company, which was notorious for seizing the equipment and ruining the film of independent film makers who would not agree to the strict licensing terms of the trust which controlled the patents of Thomas Edison and others. They were searching for locales and climates that offered more scenic options and the potential for year-round outdoor shooting. They began migrating west.

In 1909 Col. William N. Selig opened what is said to have been the first large motion picture studio in Hollywood. By 1915 studios dotted Sunset Boulevard. In 1921 more than eight hundred features were filmed in the area,

**JOHN BARRYMORE** was already in his forties when the lure of Hollywood's status and big money helped persuade him to give up a celebrated stage career. Turning his back on a hundred years of family tradition, Barrymore came to southern California in the mid-twenties. His classic stage training, along with a deep voice and dashing profile, made him a highly desirable romantic lead. Barrymore "went Hollywood" all the way, marrying young actress Dolores Costello, buying a huge yacht and purchasing a seven-acre hilltop estate in Beverly Hills from director King Vidor. The mansion included a skeet range, tennis courts, swimming pool, lots of fountains and an aviary with one hundred species of rare birds. But Barrymore was a drinker, and before long his infamous drunken escapades took a toll on his career. Suffering from lapses of memory, he relied more and more on cue cards to get through his lines. Still, he was able to walk through roles in successful films such as *Grand Hotel* (1932) and *Dinner At Eight* (1933) in which he basically played himself: an aging actor in a drunken stupor, basking in his old glory. His later films were mostly forgettable as he continued to play out his self-destructive role in front of movie audiences. He died in 1942, and ironically Errol Flynn, another Hollywood rogue whose life and career were strained by alcoholism, was pegged to portray him in the bio-pic *Too Much Too Soon* (1958), based on a book by Barrymore's daughter Diana.

and by 1926 Hollywood had become the primary center of one of America's six biggest industries. More importantly, the aura of wealth and glamour that was beginning to be associated with the movie business was rubbing off on the town. In a spree very much like California's Gold Rush, the curious and the ambitious were drawn westward with dreams of easy money and instant fame. Many of those who were lured by the mystique of Hollywood — the movie Mecca — settled and remained in Hollywood — the town.

OPPOSITE: **HAROLD LLOYD**, shown here with one of his daughters, didn't reach the pinnacle of comedic success until he and his pal Hal Roach created his bespectacled Everyman character. His very physical comedy – in which he's constantly in trouble – required endless stunt work, almost all of which Lloyd did himself. How he performed these often very dangerous acts is even more remarkable considering he lost the thumb and forefinger of his right hand during an accident on a set. He kept the loss secret from his audience with a flesh-colored glove. His most famous thrill sequence was in *Safety Last* (1923), in which he clung to the hands of a clock that was actually twelve stories above the street. There was no trick photography and only a small platform was used for safety's sake. At the height of his career, Lloyd split with Roach and started his own production company. By retaining the rights to his own films, he became one of the wealthiest men in show business, ranking with the moguls of the day, and allowing him to build one of the most elaborate mansions in Hollywood. The thirty-two-room Italian Renaissance villa in Benedict Canyon cost $2.5 million to build and included an Olympic-size pool. Lloyd died of cancer at age seventy-seven.

UPPER LEFT: **RUTH ROLAND** was Pearl White's greatest rival as a heroine in the enormously popular silent serials of early Hollywood. Thanks to her athletic prowess, Roland was able to perform her own dangerous stunts, which was valuable since stand-ins and stunt men – not to mention stunt women – were rare at the time. She dangled perilously from airplanes, leaped from burning buildings and swung from trees in the teens and twenties. Here she takes a break on the diving board with some friends (actress **LAURA LA PLANTE** is second from right) at her home in Beverly Hills in 1921.

UPPER RIGHT: **TOM MIX** hosted many Sunday afternoon pool gatherings at his home, one of the most magnificent estates in Beverly Hills. Mix had already lived a lifetime before he stepped in front of a camera. After joining the army at eighteen, he participated in several global conflicts and broke horses for the British government. Back home he became sheriff of Montgomery County, Kansas, and Washington County, Oklahoma, and was a Texas Ranger for three years. Quite a resume, that is, if you believe all the publicity from his studio. What was certain, according to journalist Adela Rogers St. John, is that "he was as elegant on a horse as Fred Astaire on a dance floor, and that's the elegantest there is." Thus, after being crowned the National Rodeo Champion of 1909 he was on the trail to becoming one of the most popular cowboy stars of all time. Mix enjoyed the Hollywood nightlife, hobnobbed with the nobility of Europe and was known to ride his horse Tony through the house to amuse guests at his frequent parties.

Beginning her movie career at age fifteen, **LAURA LA PLANTE**, pictured here in her butterfly swimcap, earned a whopping $3,500 a week, making her Universal's highest-paid actress. She gave a spooky edge to Annabelle in *The Cat and the Canary* (1927), which was the forerunner of all haunted-house mysteries. La Plante retired in the early thirties.

OPPOSITE LOWER LEFT: This aerial view of Beverly Terrace shows how undeveloped Beverly Hills was in the mid-twenties when **RUDOLPH VALENTINO** built his famous Falcon's Lair estate on an eight-acre parcel just off Benedict Canyon Drive. Valentino's property was isolated until Harold Lloyd began construction of his own mammoth estate, Greenacres, on a nearby lot in 1924.

OPPOSITE LOWER RIGHT: **JESSE L. LASKY** was Hollywood's first movie mogul. In 1913 Lasky formed a partnership with his brother-in-law Samuel Goldfish (who later changed his name to Goldwyn) and Cecil B. DeMille, an actor/writer with aspirations to direct. Their first film, *The Squaw Man* (1914) became a huge success and was followed by many others. By the end of the teens, the wealthy Lasky lived in a luxurious mansion in the heart of Hollywood. He added a tennis court and an oval pool, which were among the first in town. Despite all the trappings of wealth Lasky often preferred to ride to work on horseback.

As Hollywood prospered, the primary profiteers were the movie moguls, those powerful, visionary and sometimes ruthless producers who were the captains of the new industry. Jesse Lasky, Adolph Zukor, William Fox, Samuel Goldwyn and Jack Warner amassed huge fortunes and built palatial homes to befit their new status. To establish a Hollywood imprimatur, almost every castle had its pool. No expense was spared and no excess was deemed too frivolous. When the moguls began marketing their "star" system, celebrated actors and actresses were used as enticements to lure investors' money and attract even larger audiences to their films.

Until then actors had lived fairly nondescript lives in modest homes, but those who managed to climb to the top of the heap through talent and good looks — or by sheer dumb luck — could now take up residence in splendor alongside the moguls. Before long, Hollywood and its neighboring communities of Beverly Hills, Bel Air and Holmby Hills were studded with "the homes of the stars:" Italian villas, English manors, Spanish haciendas and French chateaux, most with tennis courts and, of course, swimming pools.

To further the myth, each studio controlled its stars' lives on screen and off, carefully orchestrating their private lives to match their public images. Even the biggest names existed in what amounted to well-paid indentured servitude. Actors signed seven-year

In 1935, **WILLIAM POWELL**, with blueprints in hand, surveyed construction of his Beverly Hills estate, standing aside his new pool. Powell started out playing villains in the silent movies, but when sound came in he adopted a suave, sophisticated yet cynical personage for detective Nick Charles in *The Thin Man* (1935). Cast with Myrna Loy, who played his wife Nora Charles, the two rode the success of the film and its sequels to great popularity in the mid-thirties. Powell was briefly married to Carole Lombard, and engaged to MGM star **JEAN HARLOW**, OPPOSITE. Harlow was first married to Paul Bern, second in command at MGM production department. Distraught over his impotence, he committed suicide, Her second marriage, to photography director Harold Rosson, lasted only one year. After Harlow's untimely passing, at age twenty-six, Powell made certain there were always fresh flowers at her grave. He later married actress Diane Lewis and the two remained together until his death at age ninety-two.

contracts that could be renewed or dropped at the studio's option. In these contracts the stars agreed to participate in the public promotion of their personalities and projects. Promotion was part of the job. In addition to selecting the homes stars were photographed in and the pools they swam in, the studios dictated the restaurants they frequented, who they dated, and even the swimsuits they wore. Real life for the stars may not have been as happy as the poolside photos – or any of the publicity shots – were intended to convey, but for a public anxious for diversion, seeing was definitely believing. As far as fans were concerned, these cheesecake and beefcake pictures proved that movie stars' lives were exciting, sexy and beautiful – as wonderful as any Hollywood press agent could dream up.

To deal with the outpouring of public interest in its stars, the studios created publicity departments whose job would be to promote and manage these off-screen images. The task entailed working as liaisons to the press, creating stories and photos that presented the actors and actresses in the best possible light. Much of the time, publicity departments cooked up and wrote their own stories for release to the press, and employed the studios' still photographers to capture the appropriate image. For the studios, masters of the art of creating illusions on film, this did not present any unusual problems.

Whenever a prominent thespian had free time, the studio would try to schedule press interviews and photo shoots. Each contract player and every movie in production was assigned to a particular press agent. These publicists went to the set daily, searching for news. On good days they concocted hot and juicy morsels that could be served to syndicated columnists Louella Parsons or Hedda Hopper, the powerful purveyors of Hollywood gossip who dished out the goodies to a public hungry for even the most mundane tidbits about their favorite stars. More substantial stories were then fed to the weekly and monthly news magazines that crowded the nation's newsstands, or were sent to the foreign press.

The best vehicles for building stars were the intellectually lightweight and glossy fan magazines, which, since they relied on studio advertising dollars for their survival, could easily be counted on to play ball with the publicists. These movie magazines, with names like *Screen Book*, *Photoplay*, *Silver Screen* and *Motion Picture*, began appearing as early as 1913. By the early fifties there were as many as thirty different fan magazines. In the period that predated television, they were the main link between stars and their legions of adoring fans. At the peak of their popularity, twelve million mostly female fans plunked down twenty cents a month for a copy and many more read the issues for free while under the hair dryer at the beauty parlor.

Many publicity photos with stars posed at poolside were originally made for publication in fan magazines and national periodicals. These very popular magazines were used by the studios to promote the stars and publicize their new releases. Fans pored over the journals to learn about the latest gossip and romantic tales about their favorite celebrities' private lives. Most of the information, however, was concocted by the studio press agents, eager to get their stars' pictures circulated.

Stories in fan magazines were sweet and folksy and focused on the romantic and glamorous aspects of stardom. Lavish photo spreads were designed to show how movie stars lived and were splashed with headlines like "Let's Go Calling on the Stars." Through these photos, the world could see for itself where stars lived, what they drove, how they dressed, how they looked in bathing suits, what they ate, where they dined, what sports and hobbies they enjoyed, and of course what was happening in their love lives. No matter that it was all trumped up – it was part of the image. Studios forbade stars to be photographed smoking or holding a cocktail, and if a screen siren's cleavage showed, it was often retouched.

This sanitized vision of Hollywood showed movie stars living the storybook lives their public had come to expect. Ironically, the smiling, carefree poses affected in the pictures often masked tragic and depressed lives the public knew nothing about. The disappointing truth was that the stars were mere mortals, and as such, susceptible to all the various human vices and temptations (perhaps more so due to their great wealth and elevated social status).

Nonetheless, they were professional actors and could generally be counted on to turn on the charm whenever a camera was pointed in their direction.

Young stars on the rise were eager and generally cooperative at these photo shoots, fully aware that these sessions were designed to boost their careers. Established stars were

often impatient and unwilling to put in as much time as the process demanded. A typical photo session at a celebrity's home or pool took about two hours, although some could run as long as three. Publicists accompanied the photographer and sometimes a writer tagged along. A photographer's assistant, a makeup person and one or more of the star's personal entourage crowded the scene, making it more challenging for the photographer to capture his subject's undivided attention. There were usually several changes of costume and locale, interrupted by breaks and makeup touch-ups. Some stars demanded that they be photographed only from their "best side," and publicists imposed additional restrictions to enhance the outcome. Legendary screen goddesses, such as Marilyn Monroe and Elizabeth Taylor, often kept everyone waiting. Some stars, like Bette Davis and Danny Kaye, could be hostile and difficult, but most photographers of the era agreed that the results were always worth the stress and inconvenience.

Photographers' rules for a successful session were these: shoot fast, keep instructing the stars – because they're used to taking direction – and get out before they tell you to quit (so the shoot ends with the celebrity in a good mood and he or she wants to work with you again). Photographers carried reflectors (and later, strobe lights) to avoid harsh, unflattering shadows cast by the sun.

**AL JOLSON** was the country's most famous singer when he starred in *The Jazz Singer*. The historic 1927 film will be remembered as the first official talking motion picture. His life story was later packaged into a bio-film *The Jolson Story* (1946) with Larry Parks in the lead and Jolson's own voice dubbed in. His wife of eleven years, **RUBY KEELER**, who is shown here pretending to photograph the lounging Jolson, was the star of many Busby Berkeley musicals. After their divorce, she retired, but made a comeback forty years later in the Broadway hit *No No Nanette*.

Such devices were essential near the water, since light reflected off the pool could make a star's face look mottled. Bathing suits were carefully selected from the latest styles (or provided free of charge by manufacturers) to best compliment the star's figure and assure the necessary sex appeal. Once the film was developed and printed, highly skilled airbrush artists could remove any blemishes or signs of aging that sneaked past the makeup artist.

Today, powerful computers allow designers to freely rearrange the visual information in a photograph, but in the Golden Age Hollywood already was quite capable of manipulating both the pictures and the print media that published them. Studio publicists, besides controlling all the elements of a photo session, could arrange for entire pool parties to materialize, get quarreling spouses to embrace on the diving board, and even find socially acceptable,

OPPOSITE

OPPOSITE

UPPER LEFT: One of the few actresses popular on both sides of the Atlantic in the thirties and forties, **MERLE OBERON** commuted between London and her home in Hollywood.

UPPER RIGHT: **PAUL MUNI**, a private person and serious actor, did his best to avoid the hustle and bustle of Hollywood. The ranch in Encino, where he lived with his wife Bela, was several miles from the nearest Hollywood mansion. Muni was nominated three times for Academy Awards, and took an Oscar home for his lead role in *The Story of Louis Pasteur* (1935).

LOWER RIGHT: **RAQUEL TORRES** starred in the film *White Shadows in the South Seas* (1927) directed by W.S. Van Dyke. Pictured at her Bel-Air estate pool in 1939, she later gave up her movie career to marry, having only made ten films.

LOWER LEFT: Broke and back in Hollywood in 1951 after her divorce from Aly Khan, **RITA HAYWORTH** tried to revive her career. A three-year absence from the screen had strained the relationship with Columbia and studio chief Harry Cohn refused to offer her a new star's contract.

gender-appropriate pool mates for single performers with other preferences. On occasions when stars were snapped misbehaving in public, studios would offer bribes to the magazines, or threaten to withdraw advertising dollars and future access to important celebrities if the pictures were not squelched. Episodes of disorderly drunkenness, arrests, drug charges, illicit liaisons, extramarital affairs and pregnancies were routinely kept out of the news. Except for an occasional unauthorized lurid picture and a few sensationalized scandals, Hollywood stars' images were as pure as their studios desired.

One person who understood the power of publicity was **RITA HAYWORTH**'s first husband, Edward Judson. Twenty-two years her senior, Judson married Hayworth in 1937, when she was an obscure starlet from Mexico going by the name Rita Cansino. Judson changed her last name to Hayworth. After he talked the head of Columbia Pictures into giving her a seven-year contract, studio mogul Harry Cohn was quoted as saying "It looks to me as if an old man has just found himself a seven-year meal ticket." Unfortunately for Judson, Rita had a habit of falling in love with her leading men, and while filming *My Gal Sal* (1942), she did just that – with Victor Mature. Her marriage to Judson ended in 1942.

In 1946 Twentieth Century-Fox signed aspiring starlet **MARILYN MONROE** and began the task of shaping her career. They had her pose for many photos like the one seen here, dropped her name to gossip columnists, sent her out for acting, singing and dancing lessons, but gave her no movie parts. A few years later, out of work and hungry, she agreed to pose nude for fifty dollars for the now-famous calendar photo that sold a million copies and earned its publisher $750,000. As *Picturegoer* fan magazine noticed at the time "she has the most disturbing physique since Jean Harlow."

The persuasive powers of Hollywood's publicity efforts not only boosted the popularity and box-office appeal of its stars, it also marked the beginning of a cultural power shift from the East to the West. People all over the world envied and tried to emulate the Hollywood style of casual glamour and wealth. In contrast to the rather formal Eastern lifestyle, with its crowded cities and harsh winters that forced more inward qualities and pursuits – an emphasis on the intellectual, the classical arts – the Hollywood way was uplifting. The West was warm and full of wide-open spaces. Life was lived outside, allowing for external pursuits – physical activity, driving, nature, all with an emphasis on action and individualism. Hot weather meant less clothing, with more attention to free movement and body shape, and more casual styles. No matter that the East saw the West as shallow, hedonistic and preoccupied with the

superficial. The world's attention was focused on Hollywood's every move; the West was suddenly the place to be.

The swimming pool became an instant symbol of this modern oasis. Its immediate association with wealth and the good life created a symbolic terrain that continues to be mined by both popular culture and the fine arts (with David Hockney's pool pictures being a prime example). It has even been recycled by Hollywood itself in many movies. The enduring classic *It's a Wonderful Life* (1947) sets its tone with a scene in which Jimmy Stewart and Donna Reed fall fully clothed into a swimming pool, setting off a poolside free-for-all that has gone on to become one of the cinema's most copied sequences. And in Billy Wilder's film noir masterpiece *Sunset Boulevard* (1950), the movie opens on a screenwriter floating dead in a swimming pool. Shot from below, he floats at water's surface, while beyond him, obscured by the murky water, looms the image of a policeman and an old Hollywood mansion. Whether interpreted as innocently portraying the good life, or drowning in its own excess, the image of the Hollywood swimming pool still resonates powerfully in our culture.

While the sad outcome of too much celebrity has been well reported in the case of Marilyn Monroe, little if anything is ever said of the others. **BELLA DARVI**, pictured here in a publicity shot for the film *The Racers* (1955), is one of those "others." Bayla Wegier was discovered by Twentieth Century-Fox's production chief Darryl F. Zanuck while he and his wife were visiting Paris. After paying off her gambling debt, they brought the twenty-three-year old beauty to Hollywood and changed her name to Bella Darvi (a combination of Darryl's and his wife Virginia's names). Zanuck then gave her starring roles in three films. In the third, *The Racers*, she was teamed with Kirk Douglas. But neither Douglas nor all the hype Fox provided could turn her into a star. When word got out that Darvi and Zanuck were lovers, she was thrown out of the Zanuck mansion and he tore up her contract. Back in France, she found some film work but by the early sixties the offers stopped coming. And her gambling debts were once again mounting. After several unsuccessful attempts in the sixties, Darvi finally committed suicide in 1971.

After hundreds of aspiring actresses
including some of Hollywood's biggest
names had been bypassed for the part
of Scarlett O'Hara in *Gone With The
Wind* (1939), an unknown actress,
**VIVIEN LEIGH**, landed the plum
assignment. Twenty-six-year-old Leigh
hit the mark with a brilliant
performance and received her first
Academy Award for her effort. In 1940,
Leigh married actor Laurence Olivier,
with whom she had made a film in
England before her Hollywood
breakthrough. Seen here relaxing in her
garden, Leigh was a physically frail
woman, and she suffered throughout
her career with tuberculosis,
exhaustion and bouts of depression.
Although she made only nine more
films, splitting her time with stage
performances, Leigh scored big again
when she played another southern belle
in Tennessee Williams' *A Streetcar
Named Desire* (1951), opposite
sensational newcomer Marlon Brando,
and was awarded her second Oscar.

Anthropologist Hortense Powdermaker, who spent a year studying Hollywood, its social structures and rituals, concludes in her book, *Hollywood, the Dream Factory*: "Of all its symbols, sex and wealth are the most important... The whole industry revolves around sex... Hollywood knows it is a sex symbol for the whole world and does its best to live up to the reputation... The other characteristic, easy Hollywood money – an enormous fortune quickly made – is the contemporary Cinderella theme... Besides these, publicity, good or bad, free or paid for, false or true, is regarded as an essential ingredient to the success story." To achieve the goal of packaging both the wealth and the sex appeal of Hollywood into a single image, the swimming pool became the essential setting.

Gathered from diverse sources, the photographs presented here have outlived their original promotional purposes and create a document of a unique place, Hollywood, in a unique period, its Golden Age. Despite the fact that they were carefully crafted to appeal to an already adoring public, the pictures, amazingly enough, maintain an air of innocence. Perhaps that innocence is just in contrast to today's magazines filled with hyper-self-conscious superstars. The old photos seem ingenuous by comparison. Although they conceal the darker and more troubling aspects of celebrity, they reveal a group of people who appeared to be enjoying their off-screen roles of living and defining the good life. We feel as if we are seeing old friends or family members in happy moments, at the peaks of their lives. But more than an exercise in nostalgia, or a trip back to gentler, simpler times, these pictures are examples of the seductive and persuasive power of visual imagery. Beyond defining a period in Hollywood photographic history, they illustrate how Hollywood thinks, works and perpetuates its own mythology. *The End*

**SPENCER TRACY** and **JOHN WAYNE** never made a movie together but they were pals. Shown here at the Palm Springs resort, the El Mirador Hotel, they are joined by Wayne's wife Josephine. Both actors got their career break in John Ford movies, but had entirely different screen images. Wayne pursued tough-guy characters while Tracy's career was marked with more versatile performances.

These two photographs appear to be from the same period, but in fact there is a gap of thirty years between them. **DOLORES DEL RIO**, a star of the twenties and thirties, is taking a swim in the pool of the home that was designed and built by her husband, Cedric Gibbons. Gibbons, the celebrated set designer for MGM, influenced millions of Americans by introducing them to Art Deco. Their home was considered a prime example of Deco or Moderne, as the style was often called in America. In the mid-sixties, **NATALIE WOOD**, OPPOSITE, found herself rolling the dice at a Moderne villa in the south of France where she was attending the Cannes Film Festival with her new love, Warren Beatty. The two had met while making the film *Splendor in the Grass* (1961), and were planning to marry as soon as her divorce from Robert Wagner was finalized. The divorce went through, but she and Beatty never made it to the altar. In 1971 Wood and Wagner remarried.

OPPOSITE: At an afternoon tea party in the pool at Pickfair, some of the pioneering talents of early Hollywood gathered around **MARY PICKFORD**. Receiving the sugar on Pickford's right is **JOHN S. ROBERTSON**, a now mostly forgotten director, who was nonetheless greatly liked and respected for his work with Garbo, Barrymore and Pickford herself. On the left, pouring the tea is **CHARLES ROSHER**, the renowned director of photography. He was an innovator in the field of special effects and also introduced stand-ins and dummies in action scenes, rather than risking the safety of the stars. During his forty-year career, Rosher was awarded two Academy Awards for his work in *Sunrise* (1927) and *The Yearling* (1946).

# THE TEENS

When the Beverly Hills Hotel was completed in 1912, it stood fortress-like over the still-bare countryside. Its guests were mostly well-to-do Easterners escaping the cold winter weather. There was, however, no swimming pool on the sumptuous grounds as patrons were not given to swimming, much less sunbathing. They chose to spend their leisure time in rocking chairs on the veranda. In the early teens, getting undressed and bathing in public was hardly appropriate by East Coast standards.

But the swimming pool took on importance shortly after a young film director from New York, Cecil B. DeMille, hopped off the train after riding it as far west as the track would take him. Breaking away from the stifling New York environment to pursue the new entertainment form of motion pictures, DeMille and his crew were searching for unspoiled scenery and year-round shooting weather. They found both in the sleepy little burg of Hollywood.

Australian **ANNETTE KELLERMAN**, a swimming and diving champion in the early 1900s, was a trailblazer long before she hit Hollywood. Known for her performances as "The Diving Venus," Kellerman began rebelling against the prevailing rigid dress code for swimwear. She told the press: "I can't swim wearing more stuff than you hang on a clothesline." In Boston, in 1907, when she introduced her own interpretation of appropriate bathing attire (an early version of the one-piece suit), she was promptly arrested for indecent exposure. The national uproar that followed caught the attention of Hollywood and she soon was the subject of a documentary featuring her swimming, diving and exercising. Before long she was starring in movies that spotlighted her aquatic skills, beginning with *Neptune's Daughter* (1914). She continued to challenge the Establishment with daring skinny-dipping scenes. Skimpy costumes like this one from *A Daughter of the Gods* (1916) made Kellerman a hot topic for years.

51

Desperate for a way to cool off after long dusty days of filming in ninety-degree heat, DeMille's partner Jesse Lasky built one of the first pools in Hollywood on the grounds of his estate and a new status symbol was born. Soon DeMille and many of the actors, such as Mary Pickford, Charlie Chaplin, and Wallace Reid, built their own pools. The pool party became a Hollywood tradition. And the pool itself was the symbol of success: the more opulent the pool, the more successful its owner.

While swimming had not yet caught on in middle America as a recreational sport, by the latter part of the decade public bathing was gaining popularity even in polite society. Americans flocked to lakes and seashores to escape the summer heat. While some would take a dip or plunge, the principal pastimes were strolling along the shore and picnicking on the sand. Early beach garb was designed to protect the body from the elements as well as provide total modesty

ABOVE: Seen here at one of Hollywood's earliest swimming pools is **CECIL B. DEMILLE**'s daughter Katherine DeMille. DeMille brought this property in Los Feliz, which in the late teens was the most fashionable part of town, with Beverly Hills still in the early stages of its development. The land contained two houses, one of which was occupied by his good friend Charlie Chaplin. DeMille had the two houses connected with a sixty-foot-long glass loggia designed by architect Julia Morgan, who is best known for her design of William Randolph Hearst's San Simeon castle. DeMille, who directed many classic films, two versions of *The Ten Commandments* (1923 and 1956) foremost among them, and played himself in Billy Wilder's *Sunset Boulevard* (1950), remained active in films throughout the fifties.

while pursuing these seaside activities. Men wore maillots, with pant legs that reached the knee, and women wore costumes with full skirts, high necks and sleeves, along with beach shoes, stockings and a hat or bonnet. Many municipal ordinances banned women from public places if they as much as appeared without stockings. Not so in Hollywood, however, where the movie star crowd was beginning to bare their bodies. Australian actress and swimming champion Annette Kellerman shocked the public with her limb-baring swim costumes as early as 1914 in *Neptune's Daughter*. (Years later, in 1952, it was fitting that Esther Williams portrayed Kellerman in her film biography, *Million Dollar Mermaid*.)

Although grand hotels and luxurious spas had begun to add pools to their grounds by the turn of the century, the very idea of a swimming pool at a private residence seemed preposterous and grandiose beyond imagination. When pictures of stars lounging by the pools of their sprawling southern California estates began appearing in the first fan magazines, the swimming pool left an indelible mark on the public. It became the symbol of stardom, and, even more, the symbol of a dream.

Tall, all-American **WALLACE REID** poses at poolside with his wife **DOROTHY DAVENPORT** and their son William. Reid established his career by making dozens of two-, three- and four reelers, often handling the writing and directing chores as well as the acting. In 1919, Paramount's most popular star was injured in a train accident. He was given morphine, which soon led to an addiction. Making matters worse, he started to drink and party heavily. When it became known that one of Hollywood's favorites was an addict, the studio had him committed to a sanitarium, where ravaged with pain he died at age thirty-two. His wife Dorothy, who was an actor as well, went on to make the anti-drug film *Human Wreckage* (1923) and toured the country leading a crusade against addictive drugs.

OPPOSITE: In 1920, four years after they met and one year after establishing United Artists with Charles Chaplin and D.W. Griffith, **MARY PICKFORD** and **DOUGLAS FAIRBANKS** were married. Having become the toast of Hollywood, the couple embarked on a storybook honeymoon before setting up a home at Pickfair. The estate soon became the elite social center for the movie world and visiting dignitaries. Aside from pool parties, an evening at Pickfair might include dinner and the screening of a new film in the living room followed by a plate of peanut brittle as a snack. "Canoe runs" were also a popular activity among Hollywood's elite, so the pool at Pickfair included a series of specially built canoe ponds, as well as a sandy beach along one of its sides.

# THE TWENTIES

By 1926, the rapidly growing movie business became one of America's six biggest industries. Movies were generating great wealth and paving the way for the lavish Hollywood lifestyle. The reigning king and queen of Hollywood, Douglas Fairbanks and Mary Pickford, had moved into their new home high atop Beverly Hills in 1921. "Pickfair" made international headlines, especially because its huge kidney-shaped pool was the focal point of many of the gala celebrations and charitable affairs the couple hosted. Partying at the Pickfair pool was as prestigious as dining

at the White House, and the pool quickly became an international social center. Guests included neighbor Charlie Chaplin, Albert Einstein, Jack Dempsey, Amelia Earhart, F. Scott Fitzgerald, Henry Ford, Babe Ruth and assorted European royalty.

**JACKIE COOGAN**, seen here with a group of friends invited to his house for a pool party, (Coogan is the smallest one) was already a precocious young vaudeville attraction when Charlie Chaplin saw his act and decided to cast him to co-star in the film *The Kid* (1921). The role catapulted Coogan, age seven, into instant stardom. While earning millions, even receiving a half-million-dollar bonus for switching studios, the little boy was given a meager allowance by his parents. At age twenty-one, his career as a child star over and forgotten, Coogan tried collecting his earnings, only to discover that his mother and new-stepfather had spent most of his trust fund. After a lengthy court battle Jackie emerged with just $127,000 to start life with his new bride, Betty Grable. The infamous case prompted the passage of the Child Actors Bill in California, also known as the Coogan Act, which was created to protect the fortunes of young actors. Ironically, Coogan is best known for his adult portrayal of Uncle Fester in the TV series *The Addams Family* (1964-1966).

Seeking to outdo Pickfair, comic actor Harold Lloyd (who had become immensely wealthy by retaining ownership of his enormously popular films), set out to build the greatest showbiz estate. "Greenacres" was begun in 1924 and completed five years later. Hundreds of guests crowded around the Olympic-sized pool at the weekend-long housewarming party, while various bands played in four-hour stints. By midweek, many tipsy couples were still found wandering around the sixteen-acre estate.

Three major icons of early Hollywood –
**HAROLD LLOYD**, LEFT, **CHARLIE CHAPLIN** and **DOUGLAS FAIRBANKS**, RIGHT – while box-office rivals, were all good friends. The three men were among the most influential, powerful and wealthy actor/filmmakers of the twenties. Chaplin and Fairbanks were partners who, along with Mary Pickford and director D.W. Griffith, founded United Artists in 1919. Lloyd's high-energy slapstick comedies often rivaled Chaplin's films in popularity.

Popular appreciation of physical fitness was on the rise in the twenties. This new attitude, coupled with the obvious safety benefit of the sport, led many to learn to swim. The Olympic gold medal performances of Johnny Weissmuller in 1924 and 1928 further popularized the sport. Weissmuller parlayed his skill and his breathtaking physique into a movie career as Tarzan. And swimming pools became a symbol not just of wealth, but also of health and fitness.

As swimming became a normal part of life, swimsuits became a regular addition to the wardrobe and swimwear emerged as a fashion industry of its own in California. Jantzen sold six hundred outfits in 1917, but by the end of the twenties annual sales had topped a million units. Its logo, a girl diving in a racy one-piece swimsuit, socks and a pompon-topped cap, was everywhere, even appearing as a hood ornament on cars. Inspired by this new craze, a young actor at Universal Studios, Fred Cole, gave up his film career and began designing swimsuits at his family's knitting mill. His became the most sought-after suits in the film industry, gracing the bodies of many bathing beauties and movie stars. *The End*

**JOHN GILBERT**, along with his fourth wife, actress **VIRGINIA BRUCE**, prepares to take the plunge into the pool of their Santa Monica Mountains home. With the death of Rudolph Valentino in 1926, John Gilbert, already one of Hollywood's most popular leading men, found himself alone at the top of the heap. That same year he met Greta Garbo, MGM's new discovery. The pair was slated to star in the film *Flesh and the Devil* (1926). It was love at first sight for the two and Garbo soon moved into Gilbert's house. Garbo preferred to spend her time in the solitude of her cabin at the back of the property. She would emerge occasionally to take a nude dip in the pool, totally indifferent to the presence of guests. Even when Garbo stood up Gilbert at the altar, he forgave her and couldn't bring himself to ask her to leave the house for another six months. Rejected, Gilbert took refuge in the bottle, thereby alienating himself from boss Louis B. Mayer. Mayer deliberately set out to sabotage Gilbert's "talkie" debut by giving him a script with dreadful dialogue. Although his voice sounded fine, his career never fully recovered. He also never got over Garbo. By the mid-thirties, with his looks, his popularity and new opportunities all vanishing, the man was in full decline and his marriage to Bruce was over. He was forty-one when he and his last lover, Marlene Dietrich, were spending the night and he suffered a fatal heart attack. Dietrich slipped out before the police arrived.

Hardly a household name these days, **LEW CODY** was a popular star of the silents and early talkies. He usually played the suave and charming man of the world who would seduce beautiful, unsuspecting women. Cody married silent star Mabel Normand at a time when her career was reeling from two major scandals. In 1922 her image was tarnished when headlines linked her to the murder of her lover, director William Desmond Taylor. After she was declared innocent, another incident ensued wherein her chauffeur was found holding her gun at the scene of yet another murder. It was the final blow to her career. The couple's marriage was short-lived; Normand died of tuberculosis in 1930 and Cody succumbed to heart disease four years later.

**CLARA BOW**, the red-headed, fun-loving "It" girl was photographed at her Spanish-style bungalow in Beverly Hills. Raised in Brooklyn in an impoverished and abusive home, the young Clara Bow dreamed of becoming a movie star. When a popular fan magazine ran a beauty contest, she entered and won first prize: a part in a movie. Her mother, proclaiming that she was headed for a life of sin, tried to cut Clara's throat and promptly was committed to a mental institution. At sixteen, Clara left for Hollywood, signed a long-term contract and became a "flapper girl." She soared to fame with the 1927 film *It*, becoming a symbol of the decade with its anything goes, smoking, drinking and dancing till dawn, liberated attitude. For the next several years Bow received an average of 20,000 letters a week, many simply addressed to "The It Girl." In keeping with her zealous screen persona, her private life was filled with numerous romantic affairs, including Gilbert Roland, Gary Cooper, Bela Lugosi and Marion Morrison (later known as John Wayne) among others. Soon nasty rumors and scandalous headlines began to appear. Before the decade was over her career was too, resulting in several nervous breakdowns. Bow spent most of her remaining years in various sanitariums and often sent out Christmas cards with the handwritten message, "Do you remember me? Clara Bow." She died in 1965.

Like many of her colleagues **ESTHER RALSTON** was dropped by her studio when sound was introduced. She continued to work throughout the thirties in a series of supporting roles, a far cry from the days when she was the star of *The American Venus* (1926). To further extend her career she changed her look from golden blonde to platinum blonde, à la Harlow. In 1941 she retired from films to pursue a successful business career and lived to the ripe old age of ninety-two.

**GEORGE DURYEA** and **LINA BASQUETTE** take a break from filming Cecil B. DeMille's *The Godless Child* (1929), which was to become Basquette's most important film. After being the lead dancer in the *Ziegfield Follies* at sixteen, she tried to make it in Hollywood. Instead she got more notoriety with her marriage in 1925 to Sam Warner, nineteen years her senior and one of the four Warner brothers who founded the studio. When he died two years later, his young bride became involved in a legal fight over his estate and custody of their child. Unable to handle the stress, she tried to kill herself several times. Relaxing here with Basquette at poolside, Duryea changed his name to Tom Keane in 1931 and starred in many westerns, then changed it again to Richard Powers in 1944 to pursue character roles.

**RUDOLPH VALENTINO** gets a hug from his wife Natasha Rambova after a dip in the pool. But things weren't always so rosy for Valentino. Looking for opportunities, the Italian, at seventeen, was penniless in Paris but somehow made it to New York where he took odd jobs and was eventually accused of being a thief and blackmailer. Bailed out by the actress Nazimova, he then danced his way to Hollywood, arriving in 1917. He landed the leading role in the hit film *The Four Horsemen of the Apocalypse* (1921). His second film *The Sheik* (1921), another box-office success, cemented his fame. With his dark good looks and Latin-lover screen presence, Valentino's phenomenal effect on women was legendary; his off-screen life was quite the opposite. By 1925, when he and his second wife Rambova purchased the famous "Falcon's Lair," an eight-acre estate in Benedict Canyon, their relationship was all but over. Valentino did not get to enjoy his rags-to-riches success for very long. One year after moving into Falcon's Lair, and just five years after his first big film, Valentino unexpectedly died of complications from a perforated ulcer, causing a world-wide hysteria among his female fans. There were reports of suicides and mass faintings, and police could barely control the thousands of grieving women who turned out for his funeral in New York.

OPPOSTE: Throughout the twenties, **CHARLIE CHAPLIN** achieved incredible international fame. Known in private life for his shyness, Chaplin, pictured here in bathing attire, strikes a coy pose. While Chaplin's professional fortunes grew, his life was never far from scandal. In 1924, just four years after his divorce from Mildred Harris (who had been sixteen when they married), Chaplin had a "shotgun" wedding with a pregnant sixteen-year-old, Lolita MacMurray. In an attempt to avoid the press, the marriage was performed in Mexico. She bore him two children, but their marriage came to a bitter end with a sensational headline-grabbing divorce case in 1927. With Chaplin's estimated net worth to be about sixteen million dollars, a settlement of one million dollars was reached. The mental strain caused Chaplin to have a nervous breakdown, his hair turned gray and he had to stop working on his movie, *The Circus* (1928) for a year.

---

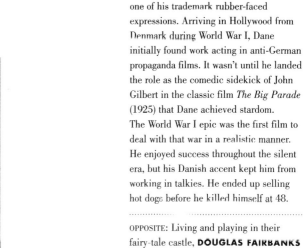

**KARL DANE,** clowning for a photo taken at L.A.'s Ambassador Hotel pool, gives one of his trademark rubber-faced expressions. Arriving in Hollywood from Denmark during World War I, Dane initially found work acting in anti-German propaganda films. It wasn't until he landed the role as the comedic sidekick of John Gilbert in the classic film *The Big Parade* (1925) that Dane achieved stardom. The World War I epic was the first film to deal with that war in a realistic manner. He enjoyed success throughout the silent era, but his Danish accent kept him from working in talkies. He ended up selling hot dogs before he killed himself at 48.

OPPOSITE: Living and playing in their fairy-tale castle, **DOUGLAS FAIRBANKS** and **MARY PICKFORD** were Hollywood royalty to their millions of fans around the world. However, the happily-married life depicted in the press was not all that it appeared. Busy work schedules and incessant traveling helped to disguise the rough edges of a relationship that was not on smooth ground. At the end of the twenties when the couple's first feature together, *The Taming of the Shrew* (1929) turned out to be a financial disaster, both their careers and their marriage were clearly on the down slide.

**GILBERT ROLAND** appeared destined to become a matador like his father. Instead the family moved from Mexico to the United States, and he ended up in the movies. With Latin-lover types all the rage, the handsome Roland quickly rose to fame. He and co-star Norma Talmadge were lovers when this photo was taken at her Santa Monica beach-front home. Unlike many of his fellow silent era actors, Roland had a long acting career that lasted well into the eighties.

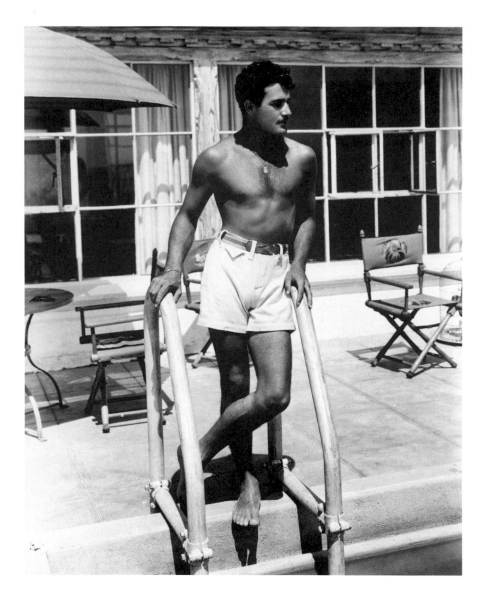

**NORMA** and **CONSTANCE TALMADGE** are two of three talented sisters who reached stardom in the silent film era. The third, Natalie, was also known as Mrs. Buster Keaton. Guided by their ambitious mother, both Norma and Constance had big career breaks by age eighteen, Norma in *A Tale of Two Cities* (1911) and Constance in D.W. Griffith's *Intolerance* (1916). Of course, Norma's marriage to producer Joseph Schenck may also have helped their careers blossom. By 1929 when her Santa Monica house, pictured here, was completed, Norma and Schenck had separated and she was facing the challenge of the "talkies." Desperate to keep her career going, Norma even took voice lessons, but her efforts were in vain. Sister Constance never even tried to put her voice to a film, advising Norma to "leave them while you're looking good and thank God for the trust funds Mommy set up."

# THE THIRTIES

Although America was suffering through the Depression, the thirties saw Hollywood reaching new creative and commercial heights. Movies were one of the few forms of entertainment most people could still afford, and the addition of sound kept theaters packed with eager and curious patrons. While many of the silent era stars faded away, a whole new group of talented actors emerged, among them Clark Gable, Joan Crawford, James Cagney and Jean Harlow.

Metro-Goldwyn-Mayer was the leading studio, claiming to have "more stars than there are in the heavens." MGM also had the most well-oiled publicity department in Hollywood, with a staff that doggedly attended to the needs of an insatiable press. Their top-notch still-photography department employed talented photographers, such as George Hurrell and Clarence Sinclair Bull, who were asked to capture the glamorous, but not-so-private lives of the stars.

As studio executives realized the sex-appeal potential of flaunting their stars' bodies, they more frequently demanded that the celebrities be

ABOVE: The athletic **RICHARD ARLEN**, who had been a pilot and a swimming coach prior to his movie career, was right at home in the water. Best known for his role in *Wings*, the 1927 World War I epic which won the first Academy Award for Best Picture, Arlen remained popular throughout the thirties, playing the durable hero in countless "B" adventure movies with titles such as *Helldorado* (1935), *Mutiny on the Blackhawk* (1939) and *Legion of Lost Flyers* (1939).

**JOAN CRAWFORD** and **CLARK GABLE** posed in a pool in a scene from *Chained* (1934), one of many films in which the two were paired. Crawford said of their collaborations: "Everything we did made money. Occasionally we even made a good picture." When her marriage to Douglas Fairbanks, Jr., was clearly failing, she and Gable, who was married at the time to Ria Langham, became "close friends," as Crawford called it. She later recalled, "Perhaps twice a week we lunched together. Occasionally we'd break away early, go for a quiet ride along the sea. And all day we'd seek each other's eyes. It was glorious and hopeless."

**GEORGE E. STONE**, top left, **MAE CLARKE**, third from left, and friends took in the Palm Springs sun at the El Mirador Hotel pool in 1933. Stone appeared in more than two hundred films, usually playing gangster types. Mae Clarke will be remembered as the face on the receiving end of James Cagney's grapefruit in the film *The Public Enemy* (1931). But a grapefruit was nothing compared to the screen abuse she suffered in a slew of gangster films. Nobody was slapped, kicked, shoved, knocked down and dragged as many times as Clarke.

photographed around the swimming pools in carefully orchestrated "carefree" poses. Swimwear manufacturers, such as Cole, Catalina, Jantzen and BVD competed fiercely to have Hollywood's elite appear in their latest designs. Bathing suit designs were exposing more of the body, and while there is no exact date when men began going topless, a swimsuit for men called "The Topper" was introduced in the thirties with a zipper that allowed the upper portion to be removed. For women, new techniques and structural materials allowed the suits to mold waistlines, make legs look longer and uplift breasts. Suddenly the stars who wore them were looking as long and lean as the trendy Art Deco beauties that artists of the time were creating.

ABOVE: **JUDY GARLAND**, at age thirteen, sits on the diving board in one her first cheesecake photo sessions. Upon hearing Garland sing, Louis B. Mayer, the powerful and intuitive studio chief of MGM, personally offered her a film contract, even foregoing the customary screen test.

**GRETA GARBO** emerges from the pool in a scene from her last motion picture, *Two-Faced Woman* (1941). After a disappointing public response to the film, Garbo quit the movie business and began her self-imposed exile from the public. One of Hollywood's biggest stars throughout the thirties, Garbo's career began as something of an afterthought. Louis B. Mayer had come to Sweden to offer director Mauritz Stiller a Hollywood contract. Stiller accepted only on the condition that his protégé, Garbo, be included. Mayer reluctantly agreed to sign her. But no one in Hollywood knew what to do with her –"too big," "too tall," "she'll never go over in pictures." When the director of her first American film, *The Torrent* (1925) saw the rushes, he acclaimed "Here is real stardust."

This new Moderne look, which was also influenced by Bauhaus, had infiltrated America from Europe and helped to redesign everything from architecture to transportation to fashion. Hollywood, quick to jump on the bandwagon, began producing films that looked sleek, glossy and, most importantly, Moderne. Astaire and Rogers danced across grand sets that became more elaborate with each new film. Busby Berkeley's lavish musicals were the epitome of the trend and very often featured intricately choreographed scenes of bathing beauties in immaculate Deco settings around an extravagant pool.

As Hollywood's most powerful studio, MGM had the financial resources to pluck the world's best talents. Among those contributing to the glory of MGM in the thirties were art director Cedric Gibbons, who introduced the Moderne look into set designs, costume designer Adrian, whose creations for the stars influenced fashion trends for years, and the mysterious actress from Sweden, Greta Garbo. Garbo, more than any other actress, fueled the imagination of film fans in the thirties. The more intensly she guarded her privacy, the more the public clamored for her. MGM executives put the studio's entire resources to work to enhance her legend, assigning the best writers, directors and designers to her films.

**FRED ASTAIRE**'s first screen test was met with a blasé reaction: "Can't act, slightly bald, can dance a little." Obviously he overcame the bad reviews. The legendary career began when he danced with his first partner, his sister Adele. Together they conquered the stages of Broadway and London, but she broke up the team to marry an English lord. Despite his famous screen test, he managed to land a small part in *Dancing Lady* (1933) starring Joan Crawford and Clark Gable. Then he was paired with Ginger Rogers and screen musicals were forever changed. Their routines often took up to three months to prep, with ten-hour rehearsal days required to perfect the intricate choreography. Astaire and Rogers enjoyed a successful partnership, making ten films together, before Rogers left to pursue more dramatic roles. Astaire continued dancing with new partners such as Cyd Charisse and Rita Hayworth. When up-and-comer Gene Kelly began his rise, Astaire retired. But the retirement lasted a short two years. Kelly, cast opposite Judy Garland in *Easter Parade* (1948) was ill, so Astaire replaced him and just kept on dancing.

And while she was known to begin each day with a pre-breakfast swim, Garbo rarely posed for publicity shots in swimwear. Ironically she had swimming scenes in only two movies; her first film, *Peter the Tramp* (1922), and her twenty-seventh and final film, *Two-Faced Woman* (1941). Her appearance in a bathing suit in the last film was against Adrian's warnings that such bareness worked against the Garbo mystique he had helped to shape in everything she wore. When the movie met with disappointing reactions, she quit Hollywood for good, leaving without an explanation. *The End*

MGM art director Merrill Pye and his boss Cedric Gibbons, the studio design chief, were among the early proponents of the new art movement called Art Deco. When Pye was assigned to the musical *Dancing Lady* (1933) he took the opportunity to integrate the style, also referred to in America as Streamline Moderne, into the movie's sets. The influence on this country's forty million moviegoers was enormous, and Art Deco soon swept the nation, redefining the shape of most interior and industrial design. While the movie re-teamed **JOAN CRAWFORD** and Clark Gable for the fourth time, and launched the career of newcomer Fred Astaire, it was **FRANCHOT TONE**, another fresh-faced newcomer, who finally got the girl. At least for a short while. Crawford, who was about to divorce Douglas Fairbanks, Jr., had fallen madly in love with Gable, but he rejected her. She eventually married Tone on the rebound, but the marriage lasted only four years.

Cutting a fine figure in her geometric swimsuit, **LORETTA YOUNG** posed on the diving board at Palm Springs' El Mirador Hotel in 1930. Young was named the official "Jantzen Girl" in 1932 and her picture appeared on posters and cardboard cut-out displays in stores all over the country. The exposure helped launch her Hollywood career and by the mid-thirties she was a major star. She initially played roles that demanded nothing more than her elegant beauty, but toward the end of the decade, and into the forties, she blossomed into a convincing actress with parts in *Suez* (1938), *The Story of Alexander Graham Bell* (1939) and *The Farmer's Daughter* (1947), for which she won an Oscar. In the early fifties, she switched to television with the successful *Loretta Young Show*, which lasted eight seasons. Although Hollywood in the thirties was hardly a pressure cooker, many stars still felt the need to get out of town from time to time, and Palm Springs' Spanish-style El Mirador Hotel was a frequent destination. Opened in 1929, the casually elegant El Mirador offered the Hollywood crowd a nearby escape where they could enjoy the desert's dry air and heat while working on their suntans. Later, during the war years, the El Mirador was turned into a hospital for wounded servicemen and it remains a hospital today.

In April 1935, French actress **LILY DAMITA**, who was an internationally known star, brought her new husband, twenty-five-year-old **ERROL FLYNN**, to the El Mirador Hotel in Palm Springs. Damita was determined to introduce her young husband to the Hollywood scene. At the right place at the right time, director Michael Curtiz cast him in the swashbuckler *Captain Blood* (1935). Before the year was out, Flynn had become Hollywood's newest and hottest star. While most studio publicists spent their time concocting romantic pasts for their stars, Flynn's real story presented a difficult problem. The press agents needed to downplay his rebellious adolescence and the fact he sailed the high seas to New Guinea, where he mined gold and managed a tobacco plantation. Instead they marketed him as an Irish tennis player and a boxer. His screen successes continued with costumed escapades like *The Charge of the Light Brigade* (1936), *The Adventures of Robin Hood* (1938) and *The Dawn Patrol* (1938). But his drinking and sexual exploits led to trouble and controversy. Unlike many other male stars Flynn, was unable to join the armed forces in World War II due to health problems. Although he was acquitted in a highly publicized rape trial, it left his ego and public image tarnished and marked a downturn in his fortunes. Flynn completed his autobiography, *My Wicked, Wicked Ways*, but didn't live long enough to see it published. At age 50, ravaged by alcohol and drugs, Flynn died of a heart attack in 1959.

Photographed here in 1932, **MAURICE CHEVALIER**, the dapper Frenchman, enjoyed two successful periods in Hollywood. During World War I, Chevalier learned English from a fellow prisoner while incarcerated in a German war camp. That skill came in handy when, in 1929, already famous on the European music hall circuit, he set out for Hollywood. Chevalier soon charmed American audiences with a series of romantic classics. A dispute with Irving Thalberg caused Chevalier to leave Hollywood in anger, but he returned in the mid-fifties with more hits like *Love in the Afternoon* (1957), *Gigi* (1958), and *Can Can* (1960). An international legend in his own time, Chevalier died in 1972.

Worlds away from his childhood in New York's Hell's Kitchen, **JAMES CAGNEY** strikes a childlike pose in the peaceful surroundings of his Hollywood home. Tough-guy Cagney danced his way out of Hell's Kitchen by portraying a female impersonator as well as other uncharacteristic roles. Cagney won an Oscar for his singing and dancing role in *Yankee Doodle Dandy* (1942). He is, however, much more closely associated with the short-tempered, fast-talking types he played in many classic thirties and forties gangster movies.

When five-time Olympic gold medal champion **JOHNNY WEISSMULLER** (seen here in a 1936 publicity photo) was offered the screen role of Tarzan, he was already under contract to BVD, the swimwear manufacturer. MGM sent their attorneys to the company to try to strike a deal. In the end, MGM got Weissmuller, and BVD got access to MGM's stars such as Joan Crawford, Jean Harlow and even the venerable Marie Dressler in swimsuits.

OPPOSITE: **WAYNE MORRIS** and his wife contemplate a swim from the deck of the pool house on the lower grounds of their splendid Hollywood estate. Morris was gaining popularity playing the heroes in adventure films when he was called into the real action of World War II. Serving as a navy aviator, he was credited with shooting down seven Japanese aircraft in dogfights, as well as other acts of military heroism. Returning to Hollywood after the war, Morris' career never quite took off again. At age forty-five, he died of a heart attack aboard an aircraft carrier while observing aerial maneuvers.

**MYRNA LOY** had appeared in dozens
of films before director W.S. Van Dyke
gave her the role of Nora Charles
opposite William Powell in the low-
budget sleuth flick, *The Thin Man*
(1934). When the film unexpectedly
became a smash hit, Loy was suddenly
a big star. Her fans voted her their
favorite female box-office draw, and
named her "Queen of the Movies."
As a result she and Clark Gable,
already "The King," were cast together
in several well-received films. After
World War II, she devoted her time to
charitable work. In 1980 she made her
last film *Just Tell Me What You Want*.

**DOLORES DEL RIO** and her dog Chow took a sunbath at her Hollywood home in 1935. Discovered in Mexico City, she was making silent films in Hollywood by the time she turned twenty. Unfortunately she couldn't avoid being typecast, so her career was limited by a dearth of parts. Popular throughout the thirties, Del Rio never garnered the kind of stardom her talent and beauty deserved. In the early forties, divorced from her second husband, Cedric Gibbons, Del Rio was frequently seen in the company of Orson Welles, who directed her in *Journey Into Fear* (1942). In 1943, she returned to her homeland and continued making films in Mexico and the U.S. She died in Mexico in 1983.

OPPOSITE: **OLIVIA de HAVILLAND**, on vacation after completing the movie *Anthony Adverse* (1936) took a well-deserved break at Palm Springs' El Mirador Hotel. After she graduated from Mills College in northern California, she moved to Hollywood. Discovered in a Hollywood Bowl production of *A Midsummer Night's Dream*, she was cast in the film version. Warner offered her a contract and many romantic leads followed. She was Errol Flynn's co-star in several films such as *Captain Blood* (1935), *Charge of the Light Brigade* (1936) and *Private Lives of Elizabeth and Essex* (1939). The two had a crush on each other that never developed into a full-fledged romance. In the role of Melanie in *Gone With The Wind* (1939) she showed new range and received widespread acclaim. This prompted her to hold out for better roles, and her studio responded by suspending her. She sued, won and was back to work three years later in a succession of great roles. At the height of her hard-fought success, de Havilland married the editor of the French magazine *Paris Match* and moved to France, making movies only occasionally.

RIGHT: Young **FRANCES FARMER**'s star was on the rise when she signed her first contract with Paramount in 1935. She then appeared in a string of features opposite Hollywood's top leading men, while concurrently pursuing a stage career in New York. Farmer, who never really meshed with the Hollywood lifestyle, made enemies of several studio moguls. In the forties, after making *Son of Fury* (1942) opposite Tyrone Power, Farmer fell into a period of severe problems with alcohol and eventually suffered a breakdown after being arrested for a minor traffic violation. With both her personal and professional life crumbling around her, Farmer couldn't bounce back. There were more arrests and convictions, leading to horrifying stays in mental hospitals. By the late fifties she had recovered enough to host a midwestern television show. She revealed her life story in the autobiography, *Will There Really Be A Morning?* (1974), which was adapted into the film *Frances* (1981), with Jessica Lange playing Farmer.

OPPOSITE: In 1935, **MARLENE DIETRICH** was photographed in the spacious garden of her Beverly Hills home. When movie director Joseph von Sternberg first saw her on stage in 1929, Marlene Dietrich was already an established actress in Germany. He knew at once that he had found "Lola" for his film *The Blue Angel* (1930). Their partnership continued with six more films; the pair moved to Hollywood and established Dietrich as a mysteriously erotic star. When their film *The Devil Is A Woman* (1935) flopped, the two parted company. In 1937, while filming in England, Hitler, who was personally fascinated with Dietrich, sent his deputies offering her fame and fortune if she would come "home" – an offer that was hard to refuse. But she did refuse and her films were then banned in Germany. Hitler's proposal spurred her to become an American citizen upon returning to Hollywood. Declaring "I am working and living in America and my interests are here. I feel I should be a citizen of this great country," she threw herself wholeheartedly into the war effort entertaining American soldiers. After the war, her career was considered to be over by the industry, but nobody told Dietrich. Well into her fifties, she returned to cabaret singing, performing all over the world, adding to her fame as a living legend. Years later, Dietrich's name is still controversial in her hometown Berlin, where city fathers can't decide whether to name a street after her.

Bachelors and house mates, **RANDOLPH SCOTT** and **CARY GRANT** were photographed together at their Santa Monica beach home, which was purchased from silent-screen star Norma Talmadge. Grant ran away from the poor surroundings of his Bristol, England home at age thirteen and joined the circus. From the Big Tent it was a circuitous route to Hollywood. After becoming a contract player at Paramount, Grant played several supporting roles until Mae West insisted he be cast as her co-star in *She Done Him Wrong* (1933). "I learned everything from her. Well, almost everything," he later declared. Soon he perfected his style as the witty and sophisticated leading man with his perfect timing and easy delivery of lines. Grant, who was equally comfortable in screwball comedies and Hitchcock thrillers, stayed on top for more than three decades. His considerable charm helped him to overshadow his eccentric off-screen dabbling with the supernatural and LSD, four unsuccessful marriages, and continuing innuendo over his sexual preference. Randolph Scott, while not as consistent as Grant, still made more than one hundred films. As a young stage actor Scott got his break in movies after a chance encounter with Howard Hughes. Starring mainly in cowboy and action roles, Scott retired in the late sixties with a fortune he had made from investments in real estate and oil wells.

To be considered a success in Hollywood in the twenties you had to be invited to Pickfair, the estate of Mary Pickford and Douglas Fairbanks. **JOAN CRAWFORD**, who at the time was desperate for true recognition, couldn't seem to get invited, so she went to a play featuring **DOUGLAS FAIRBANKS, JR.**, and invited herself backstage after the performance. Before too long the two were a couple, but she was only reluctantly accepted at Pickfair due to her reputation as a moody and driven woman with no social skills. But in spite of the naysayers, the two were married in 1929. Crawford, a poor girl from Texas, had married into Hollywood royalty. The marriage actually seems to have done more for Fairbanks's career as he credited his wife for "encouraging me to strike out on my own and be my own man."

**ALICE FAYE** stands on the gangplank
of a pirate ship, a former movie set that
she took home to her Beverly Hills
patio, where it served as a poolside
dressing room. When her singing talent
surfaced, Faye was switched from
Harlowesque blonde roles, and cast in
a series of highly successful musicals
for Twentieth Century-Fox.
Unfortunately, she had frequent run-ins
with her boss Darryl F. Zanuck, who
then hired Betty Grable to replace her.
When Grable surpassed Faye's
popularity, Faye walked out on her
contract and retired.

**W.C. FIELDS**, who rarely swam, is pictured balancing on the diving board of the pool at his Encino ranch house. In fact, he had a general disdain for water, explaining in his cantankerous manner that "fish fuck in it." At fourteen he worked as a "drowner" in Atlantic City, swimming out into the ocean, crying for help, so lifeguards could save him. The commotion would then drum up business for the carnival troupe he worked for. Fields developed a skill for juggling which put him on the road to success and allowed him to tour the world. Having performed in every *Ziegfield Follies* from 1915 to 1920, Fields then progressed to silent movies, where he further honed his unique comic style. The misanthropic character he portrayed in movies was very much a part of his off-screen persona as well: the unrepentant alcoholic who hated kids and dogs and suffered miserably at the hands of overbearing wives and mothers-in-law. He had a mistrust of cops and bankers, the latter leading him to deposit his substantial earnings into as many as seven hundred small savings accounts in cities wherever he played so he would always have access to his money.

Before her tragic death in a 1942 plane crash while on a U.S. war bond tour, **CAROLE LOMBARD** had established herself as one of Hollywood's most glamorous and brilliant comediennes. She was a Mack Sennett bathing beauty, even after she was in a car accident that left a permanent scar extending from her nose to her left cheekbone. She learned enough about lighting and camera angles to minimize its appearance. She perfected her comedic talents in a series of screwball comedies that were popular in the thirties. Her marriage to Clark Gable, aside from being an international public relations coup (David O. Selznick insisted they wed, lest they be branded "living in sin" and cast any cloud on his *Gone With the Wind*), seemed a perfect match. Lombard, who saw herself as something of a tomboy, and Gable, the rugged outdoorsman, both enjoyed life on their Encino ranch and shared interests in hunting and fishing. According to *Photoplay* columnist Faith Baldwin in 1939, "She can handle a shotgun as easily as a lipstick." She had a reputation for being a no-nonsense businesswoman, known for using language usually associated with sailors. Her death came as a great shock to her fans and left Gable crushed. Lombard's screen presence, like Gable's, remains undiminished with time.

**CLARK GABLE**, probably didn't like sitting by a pool fully clothed posing for pictures, but he was a pro and did what he was told. When Darryl F. Zanuck saw Gable's screen test for the lead in *Little Caesar* (1930) he remarked, "His ears are too big. He looks like an ape." The part went to Edward G. Robinson, but Gable went on to become the biggest male star of the thirties. Considered the ultimate he-man, Gable changed the image of the leading man, says film photo historian John Kobal: he "slapped women around with one hand and defended them with the other." The two films he was most reluctant to make resulted in his two most famous roles; the impertinent newspaperman in Columbia Pictures' *It Happened One Night* (1934) with Claudette Colbert, and of course, Rhett Butler in David O. Selznick's *Gone With The Wind* (1939). In 1939, he married Carole Lombard, who was also at the peak of her career (and earning twice as much as Gable). His life was shattered three years later when she died in an airplane crash near Las Vegas. To forget his sorrows, Gable, who was then in his forties, joined the Air Force and volunteered for dangerous bombing missions over Germany. Resuming his film career in 1945, Gable remained a bankable star until his death in 1960, which came just two days after completing work on *The Misfits* (1961). The film, which also featured Marilyn Monroe and Montgomery Clift, was the last for all three stars.

**DOROTHY LAMOUR** didn't actually get to the South Seas until she was in her late sixties. Still, the sight of her wrapped in a revealing sarong designed by Paramount costume queen Edith Head was enough to send America to the virtual tropics. She wore her first sarong in *Jungle Princess* (1936). Dissatisfied with her own, she also wore molded rubber feet that covered her flaws. Though she became known as the Queen of the Sarong, she wore the native garb in only eight of her films. It wasn't until she had been cast as the love interest opposite Bob Hope and Bing Crosby in a series of their highly successful "Road" movies that her talent as a comic straight woman became apparent.

OPPOSITE: **LUCILLE BALL** got her early break in show biz in 1933, having been noticed as a Chesterfield Cigarette Girl. Appearing in dozens of films, mostly in bit parts, she worked hard to find her niche as a dramatic actress. It was only when she took a stab at comedy that she found her true calling. In 1940, on a set at RKO – which she would later own – Lucy met and fell in love with Cuban bandleader Desi Arnaz. Ten years later, the redhead and her musical husband starred in the most successful comedy show in television history, *I Love Lucy* (1951-1957).

While it seems that Olympic swimming champ **JOHNNY WEISSMULLER** was born to play Tarzan, his casting in the role was not a foregone conclusion. Before producers discovered him for the part of the legendary ape man, producers considered Joel McCrea and Clark Gable, among others. They were about to settle for another Olympic champion named Herman Brix when the film's screenwriter saw him at a hotel pool. Weissmuller was called in for an interview with the producers and after stripping to his undershorts was offered the role. No screen test was necessary. Weissmuller went on to make twelve Tarzan movies and was the most memorable of all the actors who played the popular character. Later in life, Weissmuller got into the pool business as vice-president of the Johnny Weissmuller Pool Company.

OPPOSITE: Although she was by no means the most talented or beautiful actress of her time, **NORMA SHEARER** was nonetheless able to pick and choose her film roles, thanks in part to her marriage to MGM's vice president and supervisor of production, Irving Thalberg. Seen here in 1933 in Santa Monica, Shearer was ambitious and with Thalberg's guidance used her understanding of the movie business to claim some of the most desired acting parts on MGM's production slate. She was nominated for five Academy Awards and took the Best Actress award for her portrayal in *The Divorcee* (1930). When her husband and mentor died in 1936, she made some poor choices, turning down the starring roles in *Gone with the Wind* (1939) and *Mrs. Miniver* (1942), appearing instead in two flops. By 1942 she decided to retire from acting. She then married a ski instructor twenty years her junior and moved to the California ski resort, Squaw Valley, where she enjoyed her eight-million-dollar inheritance from Thalberg.

# THE FORTIES

To momentarily escape the realities of a world at war, Americans flocked to movie houses in the forties. Everyone was pitching in to help with the war effort, and Hollywood was no different. Many major stars such as Clark Gable, Douglas Fairbanks, Jr., Jimmy Stewart, Tyrone Power, Mickey Rooney and Robert Stack served in the armed forces. On the home front, Bette Davis, John Garfield and others opened the Hollywood Canteen, which served meals and headline entertainment to visiting men and women in uniform. Hollywood was also enlisted by the government to produce anti-Nazi films and War Bond promotions that ran in theaters along with the newsreels that preceded feature presentations.

But for the thousands of GIs who were away from home for the first time, Hollywood made its biggest impact by keeping them supplied with their favorite pin-up posters. Rita Hayworth and Betty Grable topped the list of screen sirens whose leggy pictures raised

**RITA HAYWORTH**, OPPOSITE, was a close second to **BETTY GRABLE**, LEFT, as the most popular pin-up girl of World War II. The ever-modest Grable never thought of herself as a sex symbol. In fact, she claimed the famous shot in her a leggy pose taken from the backside was purely an accident, the result of an artist needing the angle to make a drawing. Whatever its origin, the poster was distributed to GIs at a rate of twenty thousand each week. She realized her good luck, saying, "I am in show business for two good reasons, and I am standing on both of them." Her studio agreed, and insured her legs for one million dollars through Lloyds of London.

97

morale in tents, bunkers and foxholes, as studio publicity departments vied to produce the most provocative and revealing swimsuit photos. The glamorously lit, moody photos of the thirties gave way to a barrage of more basic, brightly lit "cheesecake" shots that appeared in popular civilian magazines as well as the official military journal, *Yank*.

Swimming champion-turned-movie star Esther Williams brought new prominence to pools with a string of highly successful swim films such as *Bathing Beauty* (1944), quickly becoming Hollywood's real-life mermaid. Her success caused comedienne Fanny Brice to quip, "Wet, she's a star; dry, she ain't." At the same time, swimming was becoming a national pastime. New building technology lowered the cost of pool installation so that the middle class was beginning to afford them. Pools were in demand since most of the country's youth had been taught to swim by Uncle Sam during basic training.

Hollywood was thrilled with the evolution of bathing suit design. Two-piece styles bared the midriff, and more risqué suits

OPPOSITE: By the time the public got their first look at **PAULETTE GODDARD** in *Modern Times* (1936) she was already secretly married to Charlie Chaplin, who had discovered her. The success of the film prompted Paramount to sign her to a contract, which, according to Chaplin, was the beginning of the troubles between them. After her career peaked in the mid-fifties, she retired in luxury to Switzerland with her fourth husband, novelist Erich Maria Remarque, who wrote the anti-war classic *All Quiet on the Western Front*. Ironically, she lived not far from the estate where Chaplin settled in 1953 with his fourth wife Oona, daughter of dramatist Eugene O'Neill, after being expelled from the United States.

In 1941 **ROBERT STACK** was working on Ernst Lubitsch's comedy *To Be Or Not To Be* (1942) with Carole Lombard and Jack Benny, when Benny invited him to a party. Benny's friend **BARBARA STANWYCK**, who had already established herself as a bankable leading lady, was also at the party. Stack and Stanwyck struck up a friendship that lasted until her death in 1990. When this photograph was taken at one of Stanwyck's popular pool parties, Stack was about to enter the navy to serve in World War II. His promising career continued after the war with several notable performances including *The High and the Mighty* (1954) and *Written on the Wind* (1957), for which he received an Academy Award nomination. Stack is best known as Elliot Ness, his role in TV's *The Untouchables* (1959-1963), and began narrating the *Unsolved Mysteries* series in 1991. In the early forties Stanwyck became Paramount most important star and America's highest paid woman. She created legendary roles in *The Lady Eve* (1941), *Meet John Doe* (1941) and *Double Indemnity* (1944). When her movie career slowed down in the sixties, she made a successful transition to television as star of *The Big Valley* (1965-1969), for which she was given an Emmy Award. Nominated four times for Oscars without winning, it seemed that award would elude her, but in 1981 she was given the statue to celebrate her achievement throughout her career.

While her boss Harry Cohn tried hard to control his biggest star's personal affairs, **RITA HAYWORTH** made no secret of the fact that she was living up to her on-screen image as Hollywood's "Love Goddess" of the forties. After separating from her first husband Edward Judson, she became involved with co-star Victor Mature. He was set to marry her, but there were several other suitors in the running: Howard Hughes, David Niven, Gilbert Roland, and Orson Welles. Hayworth commented on her situation: "I'm not out to corner the bachelor market in Hollywood, but I do enjoy window shopping whenever I can." She married Welles in 1943. It was clear this marriage was in trouble a few years later; when working with him on *The Lady from Shanghai* (1948), Hayworth said, "I can't take his genius any longer."

OPPOSITE: A young **RONALD REAGAN** makes a splash with his first wife, actress **JANE WYMAN** at their Beverly Hills home pool. If it weren't for a political career that began as the liberal leader of the Screen Actors Guild and ended as the conservative Republican president of the United States, Ronald Reagan's acting career would probably be forgotten. On the other hand, Jane Wyman's career was highlighted with many successes, beginning with *The Lost Weekend* (1945) and climaxing with her Oscar-winning performance in *Johnny Belinda* (1948). She and Reagan divorced in 1948 and he soon married the Wyman lookalike, Nancy Davis. A few decades later, while he was running the country, Wyman was enjoying a run as the highest-paid television actress, playing the matriarch on the hit prime-time soap opera *Falcon Crest* (1981-1990).

featured cut-out, peek-a-boo panels at the upper thigh offering more of stars' bodies for photographers to capture on film. It was increasingly common for men to be photographed bare chested, although hirsute chests were sanitized to please the censors either beforehand by shaving any growth, or afterwards by airbrushing signs of hair.

The Hollywood shorthand for affluence, poolside was now a setting where stars posed wearing street clothes as well as bathing suits, a sign that a casual, outdoor lifestyle was something worth aspiring to.

The comic actor George Burns analyzed his longtime friend's routine this way; **"JACK BENNY** walks on stage with a violin he doesn't play, a cigar he doesn't smoke, and he's funniest saying nothing." Seen here paddling a dinghy across the pool of his Beverly Hills estate, Benny made several movies – even a few good ones – although he often ridiculed them. Benny's major stardom came through radio and television where he was adored by the American public for well over three decades. Just six weeks after being introduced to radio audiences by Ed Sullivan, he began his own show in 1932, and every Sunday thereafter millions tuned in their radios and then TV sets for his dry humor and perfect comic timing, punctuated by his legendary pauses. So popular was his show that nearly every major star in Hollywood vied for cameo appearances, despite contract hassles from their competing studios. He finally retired from his television show in 1965. Forever "thirty-nine" years old, Benny took his first real violin lessons at sixty, and thereafter held concerts as fund raisers for struggling orchestras. Benny, the novice violinist, singlehandedly rescued the endangered Carnegie Hall.

BOTTOM: **TYRONE POWER** and wife **ANNABELLA** prepared to set sail on their Brentwood home pool. Tyrone Power was making the movie *Suez* (1938) when he met and fell in love with one of France's biggest stars, known simply as Annabella. When studio boss Darryl F. Zanuck learned of their plans to marry, he feared that Power would lose the adoration of his female fans and tried to sabotage the wedding plans. Zanuck ordered Annabella to take parts in a series of European productions, and when she refused, he suspended her. The couple married anyway in 1939, and when they tried to buy a home in Brentwood, they discovered that poor accounting had left him broke. Annabella ended up paying for the house until Power, who at that time had surpassed both Clark Gable and Spencer Tracy in popularity, could get back on his feet. The marriage did not produce the son he had always desired, and that, along with his not-so-secret affair with Judy Garland, strained the relationship. He served as a pilot in World War II. Afterwards, the couple tried to patch things up, but by 1949 the marriage was over.

**RED SKELTON** began performing at age seven when he would sing on street corners in an effort to help his poor mother make ends meet. Following in the footsteps of his deceased father, a circus clown, Skelton grew up performing in burlesque and vaudeville. Slowly developing his comedic talents, he broke into radio and films near the end of the thirties. He was in demand as the comic star of many of MGM's productions throughout the forties and early fifties, but found his true niche in the fledgling medium of television with his own hugely successful comedy show which began in 1951. Since his show left the air in 1971, Skelton has devoted his time to art, specializing in oil paintings of clowns.

When MGM's famous costume designer Adrian first started dressing **JOAN CRAWFORD**, he said he'd never seen such wide shoulders, and called her "a female Johnny Weissmuller." Instead of trying to disguise this figure flaw, he turned it into an asset by exaggerating the width of her shoulders with pads. When she appeared in the film *Letty Lynton* (1932), the look created a fashion trend that dominated women's style for the next ten years. Padded shoulders would also be Crawford's trademark throughout her career. Though MGM films had turned her into a star, when the studio failed to renew her contract, she proved herself immediately with an Oscar-winning performance as *Mildred Pierce* (1945) for Warner Brothers. She redefined herself for another generation in the early sixties, with her role in *Whatever Happened to Baby Jane?* (1962), co-starring with one-time rival and co-survivor Bette Davis. The widow of Pepsi-Cola executive Alfred Steele, she became active on the corporate board. After her death in 1977, Crawford's fame turned to infamy when her adopted daughter Christina wrote a tell-all book titled *Mommie Dearest* (1978), in which she portrayed her mother as manipulative, abusive and cruel. The book was made into a 1981 film starring Faye Dunaway, and gave Crawford's long and feisty career a bitter legacy.

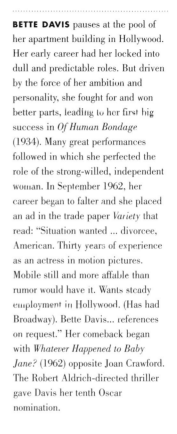

**BETTE DAVIS** pauses at the pool of her apartment building in Hollywood. Her early career had her locked into dull and predictable roles. But driven by the force of her ambition and personality, she fought for and won better parts, leading to her first big success in *Of Human Bondage* (1934). Many great performances followed in which she perfected the role of the strong-willed, independent woman. In September 1962, her career began to falter and she placed an ad in the trade paper *Variety* that read: "Situation wanted ... divorcee, American. Thirty years of experience as an actress in motion pictures. Mobile still and more affable than rumor would have it. Wants steady employment in Hollywood. (Has had Broadway). Bette Davis... references on request." Her comeback began with *Whatever Happened to Baby Jane?* (1962) opposite Joan Crawford. The Robert Aldrich-directed thriller gave Davis her tenth Oscar nomination.

# THE FIFTIES

Along with the euphoria and prosperity most Americans enjoyed in the postwar boom of the fifties came a darker undercurrent of moodiness, especially in Hollywood. For the first time in its short history, the film industry found itself competing for audiences with an upstart medium – television.

The number of households with television sets tripled as Americans moved to the suburbs, built their own pools, created the first "home entertainment centers" (consoles with TVs, phonographs and radios) and ventured out to the movies less often. Over the course of the decade, film production dropped by fifty percent. Fan magazines were also on the decline: *Photoplay*, which had boasted a circulation of more than a million in 1951, found itself struggling by the end of the decade. As Hollywood was losing some of its luster, fan mag stories turned from sentimental to sensational, and more of the "real" real-life adventures of the stars, like sex and drug scandals, were revealed by the press.

Anti-communist hearings divided Hollywood, and the emergence of a defiant youth culture, expressed through the

OPPOSITE: In 1946, retired star Norma Shearer was visiting a ski lodge when a picture of the clerk's daughter caught her eye. Shearer asked for a copy to send to MGM and a few months later, young Jeanette Morrison was in Hollywood acting in the movie *The Romance of Rosy Ridge* (1947) with Van Johnson. The film was set in the post-Civil War period, and Johnson, inspired by General Robert E. Lee, renamed the starlet **JANET LEIGH**. She's seen here ten years later with husband **TONY CURTIS** relaxing at their Beverly Hills home, both in the prime of their careers. Curtis starred in several notable films in the fifties, including *Sweet Smell of Success* (1957), *The Defiant Ones* (1958) and his biggest hit, *Some Like It Hot* (1959) with Marilyn Monroe and Jack Lemmon. Leigh was one of Hollywood's busiest actresses in the fifties, appearing in dozens of films, but none left a lasting impression like Alfred Hitchcock's suspense masterpiece, *Psycho* (1960), with its the spine-tingling shower scene. Leigh and Curtis were divorced in 1962.

A major Hollywood star for more than forty years, **KIRK DOUGLAS** was most successful playing macho roles in films such as *Champion* (1949), *The Bad and the Beautiful* (1952), *Gunfight at the O.K. Corral* (1957) and *Spartacus* (1960) among many, many others. But he was most proud of his portrayal of the tragic Dutch painter Vincent van Gogh in the Vincente Minnelli film *Lust for Life* (1956). Photographed on location in the south of France, Douglas, complete with the beard and mustache he grew for the role, took a playful dip between scenes. Back in Hollywood, Douglas screened the finished film at friend Merle Oberon's home. Among the guests that night was John Wayne, and according to Douglas' autobiography, *The Ragman's Son* (1988), the Duke took Douglas aside after the screening and confided "Christ, Kirk, how can you play a part like that? There's so goddamn few of us left, we've got to play strong, tough characters, not those weak queers."

BOTTOM: **JANET LEIGH** and **JERRY LEWIS** clown around in the pool while promoting *Living It Up* (1954), one of the seventeen highly successful comedies Lewis made with his partner of ten years, Dean Martin. In 1946 when Lewis, the clown, teamed up with Martin, the crooning straight man, both careers took off. By 1949 they were the most popular comedy team in the nation, performing on stage, television and in clubs, so Paramount signed them to do films, too. In 1956 Martin and Lewis broke up to pursue solo careers.

popularity of rebellious anti-heroes such as James Dean and Marlon Brando, created ripples throughout society. The veneer of conservative conformism and all-American family values was under attack. The public was announcing its sexual awakening with an unabashedly positive response to *Playboy* magazine and sex goddesses such as Marilyn Monroe and Jayne Mansfield.

Sensing that the public was a little weary of the "fabulous, glamorous" lifestyle angle, studio publicity departments began positioning stars as "just plain folks" enjoying their pools. But if the studios really needed to jump-start a film project or starlet's career, there was always the sure-fire, time-tested, sex-appeal angle. Though the bikini was around, it hadn't quite yet come out of the cabana. Nonetheless, fifties bathing suits, like fifties automobiles, were a product of

In the succession of Hollywood's reigning "love goddesses," **AVA GARDNER** filled the role right after Rita Hayworth in the early forties and before Marilyn Monroe in the mid-fifties. Once MGM received a picture of her, it still took another six years and a highly publicized marriage to Mickey Rooney before her career took off. She made her film debut in a starring role in the screen adaptation of Ernest Hemingway's *The Killers* (1946) opposite Burt Lancaster. Gardner is also well remembered for her legendary courtship and marriage to Frank Sinatra. She left Hollywood for good at the end of the fifties and spent a few years in Madrid before settling in London.

Seen here leaning against the diving board at the secluded Hotel Bel-Air, **MARILYN MONROE** poses for one of the thousands of photo sessions that she happily endured to achieve stardom. What set Monroe apart from all the other screen goddesses in film history was her tender-hearted innocence amid all that sensuality. As history has shown, her great success did not bring her happiness. "That's the trouble – a sex symbol becomes a thing. I just hate being a thing," she bemoaned. Her boss at Fox, Darryl Zanuck, unwilling to stray from a successful formula, kept her typecast in the same roles. When Monroe balked, she was suspended by the studio and went to New York to study Method acting at the Actors Studio. After she married baseball's Joe DiMaggio, Zanuck agreed to give her more input in her project selections. Her comedic flair surfaced in two Billy Wilder films, *The Seven Year Itch* (1955) and *Some Like It Hot* (1959). Unfortunately her insecurities and dependence on drugs, together with other personal problems, were taking a toll on her professional life. In 1962, unable to remember her lines, Monroe was replaced by Doris Day in *Something's Got To Give*, and the film was renamed *Move Over Darling*. When Marilyn Monroe, the actress, died in 1962, Marilyn Monroe, the legend, was born.

construction and engineering skills. With wire, foam rubber and elastic, swimsuits were pre-sculpted to give the wearer a curvy exuberance. Tops with foam cups created the desired pointed look (commonly called "high beams") and bigger was definitely considered better. The studios took full advantage. Even in a family photo with her husband and children, Jayne Mansfield is spilling out of her striped (or if nothing else, skimpy) bikini.

If the forties was the decade of the leg, the fifties was the decade of the bosom. The stars flaunted their breasts, and the pool was a perfectly suitable backdrop. But even voluptuous breasts, seductively displayed like mounds of diamonds on alluring padded swimsuit tops, couldn't save the old Hollywood. The days of a glamorous Hollywood where the swimming pool was the ultimate aspiration were over. And the days of the poolside photograph were numbered. *The End*

**ELIZABETH TAYLOR** could not escape the animal print craze of the fifties. It was a style well suited to her image as a beautiful, pampered feline, always on the prowl for adoration. The photograph was hyped with the slogan "If you can't drive a Jaguar, wear one."

LEFT: **MAMIE VAN DOREN** was the B-movies' platinum-blond sex kitten. Van Doren outlived all her competition and established a loyal cult following with camp classics like *High-School Confidential* (1958), *Girlstown* (1959) and *Sex-Kittens Go To College* (1960).

**ALAN LADD**, photographed in a pool-sized raft with his son David and pet dachshund Fritzie, did not appear to be the prototypical Hollywood leading man. At five feet five inches, he was too short, and his fair coloring and delicate features were not the stuff Hollywood stars were made of. But Ladd had a deep voice and a strong physique, sculpted by years as a champion diver and swimmer – both helped create a larger screen presence. His agent, Sue Carol, a former actress, was not only determined to help Ladd make it big, she married him. *This Gun For Hire* (1942) finally established him as a leading man. For the next decade he was cast mostly as a fearless fighter, playing his most famous role in *Shane* (1953). When his career faded he began to drink heavily, and at age fifty he was found dead of an overdose.

BOTTOM: **JAYNE MANSFIELD**, in an eye-popping bikini that was quite daring for its day, proves that even sexpots can have a family life. Posing by their heart-shaped pool with her two daughters and husband Mickey Hargitay, Jayne is obviously moved by the "I love you, Jayne" inscription from Hargitay on the bottom of the pool. The family lived cozily in a thirty-five-room pink hacienda on Sunset Boulevard. Mansfield's curves were first noticed in a Broadway production of *Will Success Spoil Rock Hunter?* in which she appeared wrapped only in a towel. She repeated the dizzy blonde role in the 1957 screen version opposite Tony Randall. Mansfield was an early master of the "photo-op" – her every move was well publicized. Despite her attempts to become a major star, by the mid-sixties she was relegated to working in low-budget European films, often cast along with her muscle-man husband. When she was killed in a car accident at age thirty-four, Mansfield became fixed in the public consciousness as the epitome of the 1950s American sex-bomb.

**ROBERT MITCHUM** projected a
"don't give a damn" attitude that was
enhanced by a sleepy eyed look,
the result of chronic insomnia and a
boxing injury. After being noticed in
*The Story of GI Joe* (1945) he worked
steadily in films. The self-effacing
Mitchum claimed that he became
successful because Hollywood was
searching for ugly leading men, thanks
to Humphrey Bogart. He complained
that he kept making the same movie
over and over again, the only difference
being that "they just keep putting a
different dame opposite me." Depicted
here as the "family man" with sons
James and Christopher at home,
Mitchum was the first Hollywood star to
go to prison for marijuana possession.
He survived his reputation as a "bad
boy" and many bad scripts, going on to
enjoy a large, Bogart-like following.

**GRACE KELLY** on the set of *High Society* (1956), launches a pool-sized model ship. She would launch many real ships after marrying Prince Rainier III and becoming Her Serene Highness the Princess of Monaco. She met the ruler of the tiny principality of Monaco while filming *To Catch a Thief* (1955), her third film with director Alfred Hitchcock. She managed to complete two more films, *The Swan* (1956),.and (appropriately enough) *High Society* (1956) before ascending from commoner to real-life royalty. The transition from star to princess didn't seem too difficult for Kelly, the well-bred daughter of a well-fixed businessman and a former model. Seemingly destined to wear some sort of crown, Kelly attained stardom in a regal manner: no starlet phase, no posing for cheesecake photos, and no minor parts in "B" pictures. She simply rejected all bids for her services until the appropriate opportunity to showcase her talent and charm presented itself. When she was offered a role opposite Gary Cooper in *High Noon* (1952), she accepted the part. From there she attained instant international celebrity in films in which she was cast opposite the period's top leading men; Bing Crosby, Clark Gable, Ray Milland, Jimmy Stewart, William Holden, Cary Grant and Frank Sinatra. She won an Oscar for her least glamorous role in the film *The Country Girl* (1954). When she arrived in Monaco to marry Rainier, it was only

their third meeting, but their wedding would be one of the most celebrated events of the mid-century. She died in 1982 died at age fifty-two, after her car mysteriously veered off a mountain road and plunged into an embankment, bursting into flames. A fairy-tale life ended – one that not even Hollywood could have scripted. Ironically, she died on the same stretch of road on the French Riviera where she drove with her co-star Cary Grant twenty-seven years earlier, when filming *To Catch a Thief* (1955), the movie that changed her life.

**ROBERT WAGNER** decided not to go into his father's business and chose instead to pursue a career in Hollywood. Actress Janet Leigh, who worked with Wagner in his first starring role as *Prince Valiant* (1954), described Wagner as "well mannered, straightforward, humorous and eager." These traits along with his classic good looks allowed him to sustain a twenty-year career in the movies, after which he successfully moved into television with several popular series such as *It Takes A Thief* (1967-1969) and *Hart To Hart* (1979-1984). His courtship and two marriages to Natalie Wood made many tabloid headlines, as did her tragic drowning while the two were on a boating excursion in 1981.

**SOPHIA LOREN** floats alluringly in the buff in the obscure Italian film *Duo Notti con Cleopatra* (*Two Nights with Cleopatra*, 1953), a film in which she played dual roles. Producer Walter Wanger had considered her for the lead in his Hollywood version of *Cleopatra*, but she lost out to Liz Taylor. Taylor's ex-Richard Burton said of the Neapolitan beauty, "Sophia is as beautiful as an erotic dream." Clark Gable concurred, noting, "All that meat on the bone and every ounce of it choice enough to eat!" Ironically, Loren was scrawny when she grew up in war-torn Naples, so skinny and shapeless that other kids called her *stuzzicadente* (toothpick). What's more, as she got older, she was plagued with a nose too long, a mouth too wide, breasts too big and, at five feet eight inches, a body too tall — but somehow the combination of distractions worked. At sixteen she was discovered by Carlo Ponti, the thirty-seven-year-old producer who would take charge of her career and her life. Longtime lovers, the two were officially married in France in 1966 after he obtained a legal divorce. He had already turned Loren into a major star by taking her to Hollywood in 1958 with much hoopla. Her Best Actress Oscar for the Italian film, *La Ciociare* (*Two Women*, 1961), was the first to a foreign actress in a foreign-language film. In 1991 she received a special Academy Award for Lifetime Achievement.

During **ELIZABETH TAYLOR**'s long tenure in the public spotlight, her personal affairs – her stays at five-star hotels, the six-figure diamonds she accrued and her eight failed marriages – often overshadowed her professional accomplishments. But her career was stellar – she was always cast in an important role. At age eleven she appeared opposite the famous collie in *Lassie Come Home* (1943). In her early twenties, she starred with James Dean and Rock Hudson in *Giant* (1956). Then came a string of Academy Award-nominated performances in *Raintree County* (1958), *Cat On a Hot Tin Roof* (1958), *Suddenly Last Summer* (1959), and her first Best Actress Oscar for her performance in *Butterfield 8* (1960). Taylor started a trend with her million-dollar salary for the troubled *Cleopatra* (1963). While filming it, she met her fifth husband, Richard Burton. Their highly publicized relationship was both passionate and stormy, creating the perfect artistic chemistry for their roles in *Who's Afraid of Virginia Woolf* (1966). Taylor won her second Best Actress Academy Award in the title role.

# EPILOGUE

By the sixties the elements that had made Hollywood's poolside photography both possible and glamorous were beginning to fizzle. The "studio system" which had allowed studios to control actors' and actresses' lives was

coming undone. The celebrities realized their own power and started

taking charge of their publicity by hiring private press agents. Soon the agents alone decided how, where and when their clients would be photographed. Although movie stars were still widely revered as heroes, some members of the press and the public had grown increasingly hostile and anxious to read about the scandalous and unsavory side of celebrity. The popularity of fan magazines came to a crashing halt and the glossy journals were replaced by more sensational tabloids such as *The National Enquirer*.

Three significant films of the sixties featured swimming pool scenes for dramatic effect. CLOCKWISE FROM TOP: **PAMELA TIFFIN** dancing on the diving board of the Hilton estate in Bel-Air in the film *Harper* (1966) with Paul Newman. Although the film, which was based on Ross McDonald's mystery *The Moving Target*, established Newman as a star, Tiffin didn't fare as well. *The Graduate* (1967) catapulted little-known actor **DUSTIN HOFFMAN** to instant stardom. In this early scene from the film, Hoffman, who is undecided about his future, seems isolated as he floats on the pool, even though he's accompanied by his parents. Federico Fellini's black-and-white classic *La Dolce Vita* (1960) was a view of the shallow "sweet life" of Rome's society circles as seen through the eyes of a gossip columnist played by Marcello Mastroianni. In hot European summers, a city's central fountain often serves the function of a pool by providing a public spot for a cool dip. One of *La Dolce Vita*'s most unforgettable scenes shows voluptuous **ANITA EKBERG** wading through the Trevi Fountain.

**HORST BUCHHOLZ** was known mainly in Germany and England until he appeared in the popular star-studded western *The Magnificent Seven* (1960). He appeared in several more American films before he and his wife, French actress Myriam Bru, left Hollywood and returned to work in Europe.

FAR RIGHT: After **FRED ASTAIRE** stopped singing and dancing in films, he continued acting in dramatic roles, most notably *On the Beach* (1959) and *Towering Inferno* (1974), for which he was nominated for an Academy Award as Best Supporting Actor. He also had a successful run on television playing Robert Wagner's father on the series *It Takes a Thief* (1967-1969), Astaire was photographed at his Beverly Hills home in 1968 taking a few poolside chip shots. He died almost a decade later in 1987.

OPPOSITE: **CLINT EASTWOOD** cleans his swimming pool while Maggie Johnson, who was his wife for twenty-seven years, looks on. Those were the days when he starred on TV's *Rawhide* (1959-1966). To break into movies, Eastwood went to Italy where he became a "spaghetti western" star with a slew of international hits. Back in the U.S. he continued to play tough and independent characters in westerns and the hard-headed cop in *Dirty Harry* (1971). A true Hollywood icon, Eastwood finally received critical acclaim and an Academy Award for Best Director of *The Unforgiven* (1992).

Unauthorized paparazzi photos began giving the public a glimpse of the stars as they really looked, and sometimes the results were shocking. Stars, threatened by the onslaught of aggressive photographers, started hiding behind the security gates of their mansions.

At the same time, the swimming pool was beginning to lose its cachet as a symbol of exclusive wealth. By the end of the sixties, there were more than one million pools in the United States, mostly in backyards. Parks, gyms and many motels also featured swimming pools to meet the needs of an American public which had learned to swim. For a private pool to be newsworthy required an opulence in size or design – such as the piano-shaped pool built by Las Vegas showman Liberace.

Although still popular, photographs of stars in bathing suits lost their shock value. The youth revolution of the fifties culminated in the sexual liberation of the sixties, making

images of near nudity almost acceptable and certainly commonplace throughout the western world. Bikini-clad women appeared on billboards and television, and imported European films such as *La Dolce Vita* (1960), along with major U.S. releases such as *The Graduate* (1967) more openly explored sexual themes. The few poolside photographs of stars that emerged in the sixties seemed sedate and obligatory; many were even laughably trite and old-fashioned.

In the 1968 film *The Swimmer*, Burt Lancaster portrays a middle-aged man on a journey home, swimming his way through a series of pools as he tries to find himself through recollections that each pool evokes. Hollywood in the sixties found itself in a similar period of re-evaluation. The swimming pool's prestige and the cheesecake and beefcake shots the pool had inspired gradually disappeared, in favor of something that reflected a more sophisticated, perhaps a more mature film industry. But nothing can diminish the importance of the photo collection in this book, a collection which evokes a powerful memory of Hollywood and its youthful, exuberant Golden Age. *The End*

**DORIS DAY** was such an icon of fifties All-American purity that raconteur Oscar Levant said, "I knew Doris Day before she was a virgin." By the early sixties she had cultivated a sexier and more glamorous image that flaunted the voluptuous-yet-athletic body displayed in this photo. Teamed with male leads such as Cary Grant and Rock Hudson in a string of light films, including *Pillow Talk* (1959) and *That Touch of Mink* (1962), Day was Hollywood's top box-office draw in the sixties.

# STAR PHOTO INDEX

In the early forties Howard Hughes conducted a national talent search to find a buxom female lead for his western *The Outlaw* (1943) and **JANE RUSSELL** won the part. Hughes personally engineered a state-of-the-art bra to show off her cleavage to maximum effect in the film. Russell (seen here at her home in something a little more comfortable) had to survive a lot of hype, hoopla, and vulgar jokes before she could display her real talent. The opportunity came when she starred with Marilyn Monroe in *Gentlemen Prefer Blondes* (1953). Russell was later seen on television promoting a line of brassieres in the seventies.

JEAN HARLOW

# BIBLIOGRAPHY

**ANGER, KENNETH.** *Hollywood Babylon.* Straight Arrow Books, San Francisco, 1975.

**BASTEN, FRED E.** *Beverly Hills: Portrait of a Fabled City.* Douglas-West Publishers, Los Angeles, 1975.

**BERG, A. SCOTT.** "Jesse Lasky," *Architectural Digest.* April 1996.

**CHAPLIN, CHARLES.** *My Life In Pictures.* The Bodley Head Ltd., London, 1974.

**CONWAY, MICHAEL, AND MARK RICCI.** *The Films of Jean Harlow.* The Citadel Press, New York, 1965.

**CRAWLEY, TONY.** *The Films of Sophia Loren.* LSP Books, London, 1974.

**DESCHNER, DONALD.** *The Films of W.C. Fields.* The Citadel Press, Secaucus, New Jersey, 1966.

**DICKENS, HOMER.** *The Films of James Cagney.* The Citadel Press, Secaucus, New Jersey, 1972.

**DICKENS, HOMER.** *The Films of Marlene Dietrich.* The Citadel Press, Secaucus, New Jersey, 1968.

**DOUGLAS, KIRK.** *Ragman's Son.* Simon & Schuster, New York, 1988.

**ESSOE, GABE.** *Tarzan of the Movies.* The Citadel Press, New York, 1968.

**ESSOE, GABE.** *The Films of Clark Gable.* The Citadel Press, Secaucus, New Jersey, 1970.

**FAIRBANKS, JR., DOUGLAS, AND RICHARD SCHICKEL.** *The Fairbanks Album.* Secker & Warburg Ltd., London, 1976.

**FINLER, JOEL W.** *The Hollywood Story.* Crown Publishers, New York, 1988.

**FLAMINI, ROLAND.** "Norma Talmadge," *Architectural Digest.* April 1996.

**FOLSOM, MERRILL.** *Great American Mansions and Their Stories.* Hastings House, New York, 1963.

**FOX, PATTY.** *Star Style: Hollywood Legends as Fashion Icons.* Angel City Press, Santa Monica, California, 1995.

**GILL, BRENDAN.** *The Dream Come True.* Lippincott & Crowell, New York, 1980.

**GILL, BRENDAN.** "Western Star Tom Mix," *Architectural Digest.* April 1994.

**HAVER, RONALD.** *David O. Selznick's Hollywood.* Alfred A. Knopf, New York, 1984.

**HENSTELL, BRUCE.** *Sunshine and Wealth.* Chronicle Books, San Francisco, 1984.

**KATZ, EPHRAIM.** *The Film Encyclopedia.* HarperCollins Publishers, New York, 1994.

**LAMBERT, GAVIN.** "John Gilbert," *Architectural Digest.* April 1996.

**LANCEK, LENA, AND GIDEON BOSKER.** *Making Waves.* Chronicle Books, San Francisco, 1989.

**LEIGH, JANET.** *There Really Was A Hollywood.* Doubleday & Co., New York, 1984.

**LOCKWOOD, CHARLES.** *Dream Palaces.* Viking Press, New York, 1981.

**MANVELL, ROGER.** *Love Goddesses of the Movies.* The Hamlyn Publishing Group Ltd., London, 1975.

**OTT, FREDERICK W.** *The Films of Carole Lombard.* The Citadel Press, Secaucus, New Jersey, 1972.

**PALMBORG, RILLA PAGE.** *The Private Life of Greta Garbo.* Hutchinson & Co., London, 1938.

**PEARY, DANNY, EDITOR.** *Close-Ups.* Workman Publishing Co., New York, 1978.

**POWDERMAKER, HORTENSE.** *Hollywood: the Dream Factory.* Little, Brown & Co., New York, 1950.

**QUIRK, LAWRENCE J.** *The Films of Joan Crawford.* The Citadel Press, Secaucus, New Jersey, 1968.

**RINGGOLD, GENE.** *The Films of Rita Hayworth.* The Citadel Press, Secaucus, New Jersey, 1974.

**SCHICKEL, RICHARD.** *Harold Lloyd.* New York Graphic Society, Boston, 1974.

**SJOLANDER, TURE.** *Garbo.* Harper & Row, New York and London, 1971.

**SMITH, GODFREY, Editor** *1000 Makers of the Twentieth Century.* Times Newspapers Ltd., London, 1971.

**SPRINGER, JOHN, AND JACK HAMILTON.** *They Had Faces Then.* The Citadel Press, Secaucus, New Jersey, 1974.

**STEIN, RALPH.** *The Pin–Up From 1852 to Now.* The Ridge Press/The Hamlyn Publishing Group Ltd., London and New York, 1974.

**THOMAS, TONY.** *Errol Flynn: the Spy Who Never Was.* The Citadel Press/Carol Publishing Group, New York, 1990.

# PHOTO CREDITS

**ACADEMY OF MOTION PICTURE ARTS AND SCIENCES/BEVERLY HILLS: 10, 15, 23, 41** (right), **43, 46, 51, 56, 57, 63, 68** (bottom), **72, 73, 74, 76, 84, 85, 89, 90, 91, 93, 96, 97, 100, 101, 104, 108** (top), **112** (right), **113, 118. CULVER PICTURES/NEW YORK: 2, 14, 16, 36, 40, 48, 54, 59, 62, 67, 68** (top), **71, 102** (bottom), **105, 111** (right). **EVERETT COLLECTION/NEW YORK: 18, 34** (upper right), **42** (upper right), **49, 60, 70, 82, 83, 86, 92, 95, 102** (top), **112** (right), **114, 115, 116, 122** (right). **128. GLOBE PHOTOS/NEW YORK: 107, 120, 123. ROBERT LANDAU: 26. PALM SPRINGS HISTORICAL SOCIETY: 4, 27, 31** (right), **47, 75. PHOTOFEST/NEW YORK: 6, 19, 25, 30** (top), **35, 37, 42** (upper left), **44, 77, 78, 79, 80, 87, 94, 98, 111** (left), **121** (lower right), **126. REX USA/NEW YORK: 110. UPI/CORBIS-BETTMAN: 100. MARC WANAMAKER/BISON ARCHIVES: cover, flap,13, 28** (lower left and right), **29, 33, 34** (upper left, lower right and left), **42** (lower right), **50, 52** (right), **55, 58, 61, 64, 65, 66, 69, 103, 108** (bottom), **124. DICK WELLS: 99.**